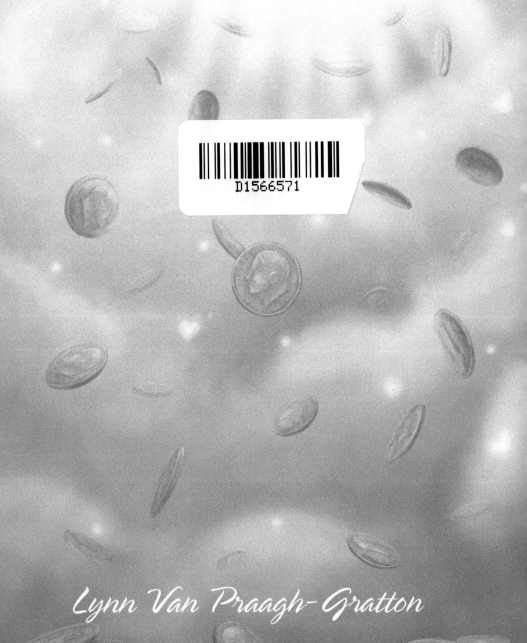

DIVINE DIMES

Messages of Love and Healing from
BEYOND

D1566571

Lynn Van Praagh-Gratton

"The Times They Are A-Changin'"

. In 1963, Bob Dylan's poetic voice delivered a reverberating somber warning in a song titled "The Times They Are A-Changin'." And, today, I sense a similar urgency of concern about tomorrow's destiny and the need for each of us to reflect upon life's purpose and to tailor our actions accordingly.

Dylan's lyrical verse began:

> Come gather 'round people
> Wherever you roam
> And admit that the waters
> Around you have grown
> And accept it that soon
> You'll be drenched to the bone.
> If your time to you
> Is worth savin'
> Then you better start swimmin'
> Or you'll sink like a stone
> For the times they are a-changing.

What "waters" have grown since 1963? Quite literally...our oceans! Greenhouse gases are heating the Earth's atmosphere and the Arctic is warming at twice the rate of the rest of the planet; Greenland ice sheets are melting; and two vast glaciers in East Antarctica, which make up two-thirds of the continent, have been losing mass rapidly since 2002...all causing the rate of sea levels to rise signaling foreboding consequences. We are also experiencing more violent storms and ravaging fires which are sending a warning message about an uncertain future for Mother Earth and for those who call it their home.

Figuratively, the "waters" have grown as well. We, as a community of nations, are facing nuclear arsenals expanding at an alarming rate with fingers crossed that some madman won't decide to use them one day; drug-resistant infections now threaten a worldwide pandemic causing a global catastrophe unlike ones experienced in recorded history; religions are in crisis and beliefs are being contorted to justify extreme acts of cruelty deprived of a conscience; political rancor is now the order of the day treading upon the coattails of civility at the expense of compromise and reconciliation.

Dylan fundamentally asked two questions that are central to the reason why I wrote this book and asked you to read it with an insightful mind.

> If your time to you
> Is worth savin'
> Then you better start swimmin'
> Or you'll sink like a stone.

Hopefully, once your fingers reach the final page captioned "Epilogue," I will have brought you closer to an answer about the purpose behind your "time" spent on the third planet from the Sun and in what direction you need to start "swimmin'" if you are to avoid sinking like a stone.

Special thanks to
BRETT STEPHAN
BASS
*for helping
to weave my thoughts
into a tapestry.*

Opening my heart to let love
abundantly flow, I dedicate this book to...

My Children:
>Dennis Michael
>Gail Lynn
>Christopher Gary
>Gregory Matthew

My Grandchildren:
>Brittany
>Gianna
>Alyssa
>Kiley
>Kayden
>Alex
>Dominic

And:

The eternal light of my life, my soul mate,
Dennis, who allowed my heart to sing with
joy and to truly experience the purity of the
word "LOVE."

The true essence of the human spirit is fleetingly encased in a chrysalis of flesh.

Death releases it so that it can escape its momentary confinement, allowing it to soar and be welcomed and embraced by "eternal love."

My Journey Is Your Journey

For many years, I have yearned to compose my biography. Why? To leave a living memorial of my work and life experiences intended to be handed down from one generation to the next so that my children... grandchildren... and great-grandchildren will intimately come to know me and to assure them that my loving energy will always be with them even though they may no longer be able to see me or to physically touch me.

Before I began to consider assembling the thoughts needed to piece together my life story, I went to a local Long Island beach to ask the eternal energy of the universe, which I have come to know as the "Source," to allow me to begin a journey of remembrance and to share my life experiences with others. Perched on a rock in a secluded spot where few deemed worthy of visiting, I gazed upon the stillness of the Atlantic Ocean, having crossed it many times to travel to Europe. Suddenly, I found my mind at peace with the cosmos.

As a solitary gull flew overhead with lightning speed, it triggered my memory and I recalled what my father had told me as a very young child..."The older you get, the faster time seems to travel." And, the urgency of writing this biography became a pressing priority when I recalled his words.

With pad and pen, I have now returned to that isolated rock to begin to piece my thoughts together, inviting you to sit beside me and to accompany me on a journey of understanding because, as you will discover, my journey is really your journey... a journey that ends when we all become "One With The SOURCE!"

Our Spiritual Journey

Finding Dimes

Look down, not up! Has a dime lying on the ground captured your attention…found its way into your hand…been deposited into your pocket? If so, you are not alone in experiencing what others have found, at times, confounding.

In countless spiritual healing sessions that have spanned my lifetime, people have often recounted finding a dime here or a dime there abandoned in the strangest place or places. "What is the meaning?" I am frequently asked. "A message? Serendipity? The misfortune of another? A chance encounter with fate authored by the celestial cosmos?"

Experience has tutored that chance, while plausible, may not always be the case. Rather, the finder is meant to find it! Meant to find it? Why? Left by whom? Consider these explanations that my spiritual guides have revealed to me to quench my yearning thirst to know:

> *In a place which I call "Beyond the Beyond," where the energy of our consciousness resides after death, someone is reaching out to us.*

Why? Most often:

> *A deceased loved one wants to gain your attention to let you know that he or she is around you.*

Why? Most often:

> *To reassure you that he or she has survived the process of physically dying and that the love that*

i

he or she shared with you on our earthly plane of existence continues on. And, to watch over you.

How? Most often:

To reach into your subconscious mind and provide guidance that counsels whether life decisions about to be made will be in your best interest. However, the ultimate choice still resides with your conscious decision-making.

The dime also reminds us to keep our eyes wide open…not be distracted from the tasks immediately at hand or, more profoundly, it harks back to the number 10 which spiritually represents a full circle indicating that you have or are about to complete an important task.

To ancient cultures, the number 10 was vested with divine inspiration. Biblically, there were 10 Commandments, 10 nations, 10 plagues that ravished Egypt, and, in Christianity, the Holy Spirit descended on the apostles 10 days following the Ascension of Jesus. Pythagoras of Samos (570-495 BCE), an Ionian Greek philosopher and mathematician, valued the number 10 as the representation of the universe and the totality of cosmic knowledge. The Mayas interpreted the number 10 cyclically…the end of one cycle and the start of the next…essentially, the dance of life and death.

The title of my biography, "Divine Dimes," resonates with me because I have been showered with many dimes that have appeared unexpectedly at my feet to offer reassurance that my life's journey is blessed with purposeful meaning. They have connected me, and continue to connect me, with my beloved husband, Dennis…my mother, Regina ("Jean")…my father, Allan…and other relatives who watch over me from **Beyond the Beyond** conveying inspiring love. They connect me to my first **Spiritual Master Teacher,**

Chief Red Cloud, and other guides who will be referenced in this book and who provide the tools that allow me to achieve my pre-ordained life's purpose…to bring comforting healing messages to those who grieve the loss of one who once enriched their lives.

Know that I don't know how dimes are manifested. All I do know is that my psychic-medium gift is a testament to the realization that what seems, at first glance, unbelievable, is invested with a purpose emanating from an eternal caretaker who I have come to know as the **Source**.

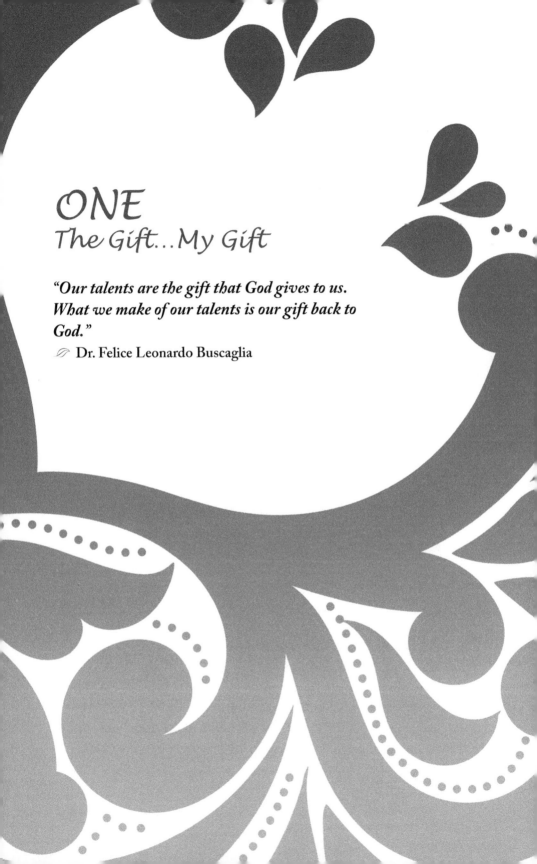

ONE
The Gift...My Gift

"Our talents are the gift that God gives to us. What we make of our talents is our gift back to God."

✎ Dr. Felice Leonardo Buscaglia

A poet's eyes and mind peer into a nighttime panoply of stars without the aid of a telescope and is rewarded with boundless inspiration that is captured by transcendent verse. A child prodigy climbs onto a piano bench and her fingers instantly create a soothing melody that resonates with the heartbeat of the universe. The artist's brush dances effortlessly on a canvass to bring two dimensions into a three dimensional world to enliven mankind's sensual senses.

Some are born to be a craftsman to use a chisel to fashion beauty from a lifeless block of wood or shapeless discarded stone. Some are born with a voice that can enslave a room, stilling and then titillating the emotions of others. Some are proficient in conquering complex mathematical equations…some have an attentive ear that can absorb languages like water easily drawn into a sponge… some find themselves with the embedded skills of an athlete easily translated into a celebrated professional career. Why Einstein? Why Shakespeare? Why Michelangelo? Why Beethoven? Why the King of Swat, Babe Ruth? Why a psychic-medium born with the "gift" of receiving words conveyed by the departed?

The quote that underscores this chapter bears repeating… "Our talents are the gift that God gives us. What we make of our talents is our gift back to God."

We may all have a different understanding of what the word "God" means based upon our ancestral heritage, contemporary culture, or parental upbringing. For me, the word "God" has been replaced by the word *Source*, and, through my healing work, I have come to know the *Source* as the eternal repository of *"love, knowledge, wisdom,* and accepting understanding bathed in the *purity of celestial light."* So, humility dictates that I take no credit for the gift that accompanied my birth. The source was from the *Source*. But, what use I make of it is up to me. And the worth of my life, when it has ended, will be measured by whether the gift was embraced to be shared with others or was needlessly squandered to lie fallow like an uncultivated patch of barren earth.

A lady doesn't like to advertise her age. So, suffice it to say that touching up gray hairs is sometimes necessary. Why introduce the subject to begin with? To allow you to appreciate that a lifetime of being a psychic-medium, during which time I've tried to grasp its insightful purpose, has provided glimpses into the true meaning of life and the architecture which has shaped our *spiritual* universe. While I certainly don't profess to know most of the answers, the path I've followed in life has provided hints along the way which I am blessed to share with you.

When I reached the tender age of four, in looking back, I can vividly recall being bathed in **happiness** and **joy** that embraced me. It wasn't the traditional love carried from a mother's and a father's heart to their firstborn child. No! It was stronger than a maternal and paternal connection! It was far more powerful! It was meant to be far more enduring! I didn't appreciate this inner feeling of **profound love** until my years advanced from childhood and arrived at adulthood when I realized that the author of this overwhelming feeling of contentment was the **Source**.

What is the **Source**? There is a simple answer bathed in perplexing complexity: "The **Source** is the **purity of love** represented by the **purity of light**!" It is an *energy source* that arrived with the birth of our universe or with what physicists speculate may even be a multiverse of countless universes. How was the **Source** created? I don't have the wisdom to know. All that I can report with confidence from years of personal experience is that it does exist and is timeless. And, most importantly, we are all born with a piece of the **Source** within ourselves to, one day, reconnect to the "**oneness**" of the universe— that "**oneness**" being the **Source**.

Who am I? Who are you? **Energy** or **modulating frequencies** residing in a human body that will survive once we shed our mortal flesh. Is it our *consciousness* which science to this day cannot adequately explain?* Is it mind separate from body intended to eventually advance to a higher *energy-frequency realm*? I believe so. Those who have experienced a near-death event often recall, in vivid detail, looking down and seeing their seemingly lifeless corpse, only to suddenly return to reengage in life with the experience tattooed to their memory—*mind-energy* able to survive without the need of a physical body!

A question which I am constantly asked is: "What is the purpose of life?" It is a profound query which has plagued mankind since the first eyes peered into the night sky and viewed the firmament with wonderment. Drawing on my many decades as a psychic-medium, I have come to believe that the word purpose can be translated to mean "perfection." We are here on this earthly plane of existence to achieve "a perfect harmony with the *Source* so that we can be prepared to become '*one*' with the *Source* and experience the purity of *eternal love* for immeasurable time." It's like you are the tuning knob on a radio. The *Source* is trying to talk to you but there is too much static interference coming through the speakers. What do you do? You gently turn the knob until the voice is crystal clear.

Thus, to repeat. "What is the purpose of life?" To adjust your *energy* or *frequency* knob to align it to that of the *Source's*. "How?"

---

* **Consciousness** is what makes you…you! It allows you to appreciate the redness of red in a bouquet of long-stemmed roses; the ecstasy of romantic love; the agony felt at a gravesite; and all of the other subjective feelings we experience in life. Yet, consciousness is a mystery to science. The *International Dictionary of Psychology* describes it in these words: "…a fascinating but elusive phenomenon; it is impossible to specify what it is, what it does, or why it evolved. Nothing worth reading has been written about it."

you ask. Fasten your seatbelt because you're in for a bumpy explanation ride that may conflict with your current thinking!

Can you go to college without attending nursery school... elementary school... junior high school... then high school? Knowledge and wisdom built over years lay the groundwork for an advanced education. Thus, to become *"one"* with the **Source**, there is a path which we all must follow... step by step by step. And that involves *"reincarnation"* intended to achieve "a perfect radio frequency signal that allows us to align with that of the **Source's**."

Doing countless readings to channel those who have passed, I've learned that we are born and reborn with a design plan in mind. Each time we breathe life, we have been pre-programmed to learn a *new* life lesson or lessons. Lessons are building blocks. Perhaps we are here to experience the depth of joy or the heartbreak of pain and loss; or to develop empathy and to appreciate the bountiful blessings delivered by charitable giving; or to mentor others; or.... Look into the mirror and ask yourself: "What has life taught me? What life lesson or lessons have I learned and what do I need to learn to become a better person...a *more perfect energy* that can tune into the **Source's** frequency?"

Personally, I know that I will be reborn again. I feel it in my spiritual gut. Would I prefer to become *"one"* with the **Source** now? Yes, of course! However, my **Spiritual Master Teacher** has told me that: "My destiny will arrive when it is meant to arrive. And that that time has not yet come."

"Spiritual Master Teacher?" you may question my strange reference. Well, I'll introduce you to him in the next chapter. But, for this moment, let me reassure you that, like me, you are not alone in this present incarnation. Others having a higher energy or frequency are with us to offer *protection*, *guidance*, and *understanding*. Really? Yes! Who are they? How do they communicate with us? Do we listen to them... if not, why not?

The **Source** has dispatched guides to help elevate our energy since we can't do it alone. They can be few or many depending upon how much our energy levels have grown over a series of life-times. Suffice it to say that you have a *Spiritual Master Teacher*, *Earth Guides* who once lived on this earthly plane, and *Celestial Guides* who have never lived on earth. Each has been assigned a task that relates to your life. How do they communicate with you? Through your **subconscious mind** manifested as a "gut reaction" or what's called "intuition." You tell yourself: "There's something here that doesn't seem right," and you avoid a danger. "I don't trust that person," because an inner voice conveys a warning.

Guides, however, can't always intervene to eliminate life's mis-steps. You do have free will! A subconscious message may be ig-nored by your conscious awareness. Remember when your mother told you to take an umbrella with you because rain was predicted. And? You ignored her advice. Well then... you got soaked! Guides can only do so much. Decisions, good and bad, reside within you to make.

As a psychic-medium, I can connect you with your departed loved ones employing my channeling gift. But know that you can connect as well by meditating, by paying attention to your dreams, by sending thoughts and prayers of love to those residing *Beyond the Beyond*, and by looking for signs left by the departed to let you know that they are around you... dimes deposited at your feet; items moving on a table in your home; a scent that reminds you that he or she once wore a certain perfume or shaving cologne; a license plate in a parking lot that draws your attention because the numbers or the letters resonate with meaning; etc.

As you read further, many of the things that I have mentioned here will be expanded upon. I have introduced them to whet your appetite to read on and to know more. But first, let me introduce myself to you in greater detail in the ensuing chapter titled "Why Me?" so that you can measure and weigh the strength of my words and their profound message.

TWO
Why Me?

"Why me?" she asked, holding on to him.
"Because you cared," he whispered.
"You cared so much for your people."
Annette Curtis Klause

Your hair is blond and not black. Your eyes are blue-green and not brown. Your fingers are long but your toes are short. Your skin tone is fair. You're way above average in height. You have dimples and freckles. Why? Inheritance!

When you gaze into a mirror give credit or blame to your parents for the reflected image that is staring back. Your hair color was inherited from your parents. It is the result of the absence or presence of two types of melanin, either eumelanin, which is the author of brown and black hair, or phaeomelanin, which produces red or blond hair. You have freckles because one or both parents do. The same holds true for your dimples. And the list goes on and on and on.

A psychic-medium! *Why me?* As you accompany me on my life's journey in this chapter, you will learn that our understanding of the word "inheritance" is incomplete in its traditional meaning. Not limited to physical appearance, it captures more than the naked eye can see. In my case, my gift of channeling words from the other side of life was inherited from my mother, Regina, and my Great-Aunt, Maggie O' Day. And, I have passed it on to my son, Dennis J.

So, I received an extraordinary gift. The "how" is clear, "inheritance," but the "why" is somewhat cloudy. As you will learn as my story unfolds, my mother lived a tormented life because she couldn't make sense, or come to grips, with her psychic-medium gift. It proved to be like Coleridge's ancient mariner, an albatross around her neck with the weight causing her to lose her footing and stumble in life. As my years unfolded, I began to understand, and then appreciate, my spiritual inheritance. If only I could have shared that wisdom with my mother to turn her despair into joyous celebration. But fate regrettably had other plans...perhaps to teach me a life lesson!

The "why" which eluded my mother has found purpose in my life and brought comforting satisfaction to my heart. I have become a ***healer*** and a ***teacher*** meant to wipe away tears from the eyes of parents who have lost a child…a spouse who has lost his or her soul mate…the heartbreak brought about by the passing of a lifelong friend. I take no credit for the gift which greeted me when I took my first breath. But, I do cherish the opportunity to use it wisely to connect the living with those who have left behind only memories, and to provide reassurance that physical death is not an ending but rather the beginning of a new journey for all of us. "*Why me?*" as the chapter's introduction states? Because, I truly **care** about the **people** who continue to grace my life!

"Credibility", the way we are perceived and are believed, is a sacred word. How do we value another person's story? By getting to know someone and then excavating into their character to extract the word "integrity." If the words in this book are to carry weight and merit, then, to earn your trust, I need to share my past in order to give meaning to my present. So, allow me to recite from my memory scrapbook.

My mother, Regina ("Jean") F. McLane, and my father, Allan L. Van Praagh, were married in Manhattan, New York; she, age 29, and he, four years her junior. For a time, my mother worked for Walt Disney Productions in New York City as, believe it or not, Walt Disney's private secretary!

My father's side of the family traced their lineage to those speaking Dutch with a sprinkling of Welsh mixed in for good measure. My mother, by contrast, had roots honoring the Irish and their marvelous heritage.

For my mother, religion was the linchpin of her life having been raised in a strict Irish Catholic household. Dutifully, she carried these traditions in her mind and in her heart and applied them to our day-to-day lives. With a powerful connection to the Blessed Mother Mary, and especially to St. Thérèse of Lisieux, popularly called "The Little Flower of Jesus" or just "The Little Flower," my mother embraced religion with an inexhaustible passion that never faltered.

Throughout her adult life, my mother cast her eyes skyward beseeching the heavenly "Little Flower of Jesus" to help her cope with mounting times of despair. Sadly, despondency often intruded into my mother's life, stalking her with all the ferocity of a lion on the prowl desperate for a meal. Like a medicinal elixir intended to comfort an aching heart, Regina Van Praagh would tutor: "If you ever feel alone or need help, then offer this prayer to St. Thérèse…*'Little Flower in this hour, please show your power'*." In the same spirit of acceptance, I too grew to love the imagery of one who sacrificed much to help others and, as a testament to my own personal devotion and commitment, I proudly took Thérèse's name as my confirmation name.

While mother was a devout Catholic, my father was raised as an Episcopalian which did not sit well with my mother. In her mind, if you swayed an inch from her chosen faith then you might as well be a heathen. This religious difference would be a smoldering cauldron of tension sitting on our family hearth throughout my upbringing.

When my father exchanged marriage vows, he came to the marriage with the grandest hopes, dreams, and ambitions. Like "The Little Flower," he chose service to his community, donning the uniform of a New York City police officer. But, destiny was unkind to his desires. Diagnosed with type 1 diabetes two years after joining the force, the stress of the job played havoc with his disease and the predicated long-term consequences to his health became painfully real. Thus, my father surrendered to necessity and traded his dress blues for less formal attire and a different form of "less stressful" excitement. He became a stagehand for television and Broadway productions becoming a member of Local 1 of the I.A.T.S.E. (International Alliance of Theatrical State Employees), adding to a family legacy that would span 122 years.

During the course of his work, my father met scores and scores of celebrities and stars in the making. I could go on and on and on describing his encounters with so many different personalities whose emotions ran the gamut…sad, happy, whimsical, humorous, and, occasionally, tragic.

Although Allan L. Van Praagh, my beloved father, was thrown off of life's intended path by a serious genetic health issue, I am proud to recall that he never complained or bemoaned what might have been judged to be fate's cruel injustice. He confronted life with reborn perseverance.

Wishes and expectations were not so easily fulfilled for Regina and Allan and, as time marched along, they voiced a growing concern. They wanted to celebrate the arrival of a firstborn, but somehow nature was resistant, refusing to cooperate. So, my mother sought a physician's opinion, and, after a pelvic examination, his answer was disquieting. The haunting diagnosis was a "retroverted uterus," or "tipped uterus," which occurs when the uterus is tipped backwards towards the spine. In the vast number of cases reported, the cause has its origin in genetics.

According to my mother, the doctor offered a grim assessment for her chances of conceiving a child. In his words, denied of compassion, he said: "The condition that I have found Mrs. Van Praagh is most uncommon. Likely, you'll never conceive a child." His advice: "Try sitting in hot baths to see if the abnormality improves."

The advancement of science and medicine has been astounding but, at the time, few options were available to my mother to correct the condition and to welcome the arrival of a healthy fetus. So, what did my mother do? Night after night after night she soaked in a hot bath praying to St. Thérèse of Lisieux to send a beating heart to her womb. And her prayers were finally answered months later.

What an extraordinary woman my mother was to persist and persist and persist unwilling to surrender to the doctor's bleak prediction. For that perseverance, I express gratitude sketched by the most vibrant colors of the rainbow.

Confirming what she had already sensed— that she was incubating a precious life— my mother once more consulted her physician who confirmed her self-diagnosis. Again, however, he would prove to be wrong. "The baby will come on our nation's birthday....July 4th," he said with a renewed reassurance. Well, *I* didn't cooperate. It was June 29th when my loving parents held me in their arms for the very first time. And, thereafter, three siblings followed in succession, eventually expanding our family to six.

Thus, just as summer replaced spring, Lynn Elizabeth, (**me**!), was joined with the Van Praagh surname. I don't know why my parents chose Lynn, but I suspect that it relates to my father's sprinkling of Welsh in his bloodline. You see, Lynn is an English family name which is derived from Welsh "llyn lake." As for Elizabeth, it honors my paternal grandmother, Ethel Burrows-Van Praagh, who was English. Therefore, my middle name pays tribute to the Queen of England. But, believe you me, royalty I'm not!

Since the day I was born, I have lived an unpretentious life without a driving urge prodded by materiality. Growing up, my family lived in a modest home in Bayside, Queens, New York. These humble surroundings, you need to know, enriched my life with middle-class values which have helped to mold and to shape the woman who I have become.

For the most part, childhood memories that advance way back in time tend to be few for most of us, unless, of course, they leave what Thoreau called a "mindprint." And I can recall, with all the vividness of it occurring yesterday, such a transformative event in my life when I barely crept past my third birthday.

My family was having dinner with my Aunt Catherine and my Uncle Stubby, a delightful nickname, in our Bayside home. The air was so thick it could be sliced with a proverbial knife, and black foreboding clouds promised an arriving summer storm. And then it came...thunder and lightning that rattled our windows and teased and tested our nerves and fragile emotions.

Reliving the experience, I remember being a frightened child as the storm introduced its fury. The thunder claps terrorized me, and I'm sure that my little body must have been quaking and quivering at the time because I recall that my Uncle Stubby had placed me on his knee by a window overlooking our small grassy backyard and embraced me to provide comforting reassurance that things would be all right.

And then it happened! A blinding lightning bolt slammed into the ground outside that picture window and an odd sensation consumed my emotions. I know this seems strange, even bizarre, but I assure you it was so real that the memory has attached itself to me like a haunting shadow. The light that violently exploded before my eyes made me feel as though it had "traveled through me." And then…and then…I sensed, or somehow knew, that there had been some sort of shapeless form in the flash of light the moment that it struck the ground. In retrospect, I would describe the figure as "translucent without gender."

How did that day alter my life? With a mixture of both joy and fear, if the truth be told. Since that day, I carry within my psyche an aching anxiety about thunder and lightning. I guess most people do, especially young children who have had early memories of an event that proved to be traumatic. But, strangely, while I fear the ferocity of thunder and lightning, I have also grown to love it as well. Why? Because that early childhood event changed my life, not for a fleeting moment but rather for forever! It somehow tutored that in **light** there is **love** and some deeper celestial meaning, perhaps leading to a pathway to **Beyond the Beyond** in a realm on the other side of earthly life, an astral plane of existence.

Did I mention this event at the time to Uncle Stubby, or years later to anyone else? No! Why? I believe it was out of an innate fear of being disbelieved or, far worse, being misjudged and labeled with an unkind pejorative adjective.

Two years later, at age five, our family traveled 313 miles upstate to Dansville, New York, during the summer, for a short vacation to spend time with our extended family—my maternal grandmother,

Katherine D. McLane, and cousins. Dansville, a sleepy little village in the eastern part of Livingston County, got its name from Daniel Faulkner who settled in the area in 1795. No doubt the village's greatest claim to fame is that Millard Fillmore, our 13th President, resided in Dansville for several months.

In an upstairs bedroom, my cousin, Ruth, and I were playing as a light rain began to fall. Suddenly, like an unexpected stranger banging on the door to shock those tending to their business inside, an electrifying ball of lightning struck the ground in front of the house. The sky lit up like a Fourth of July fireworks celebration and the house rumbled. Quickly, my eyes were drawn to the window and, once again, I perceived a shapeless specter in the pillar of light. Vividly, I remember asking my cousin whether she had seen what I had seen. Her reply was "No!" And, for a child of five, the lack of confirmation was unnerving. "What's wrong with me?" I questioned myself. Thereafter, apprehension intruded into my life and I decided to keep my observations quietly within.

In addition to having relatives living in Dansville, New York, I also had cousins residing in Rochester, New York. When our family visited them, I slept in a room that had a maroon rocking chair that had been passed down from generation to generation, originally belonging to my great-grandmother who had long since passed to the other side. Strangely, each time I visited Rochester, and each time I slept in the same bedroom, out of nowhere, the rocker would begin to sway back and forth. Was I frightened? Surprisingly not! Something within my heart of hearts reached deep into the fiber of my being and told me to be still and to feel peacefully at ease. Why were my emotions composed and tranquil? Because, from ***Beyond the Beyond***, the energy of my deceased Great-Aunt Maggie O' Day had come to pay me a visit and, as a child, I somehow received her presence with a soothing calm.

My Great-Aunt Maggie was a gifted psychic, a trait that blazes a path straight through my mother's lineage. Not to jump too far ahead, let me just say that my mother had the gift. I have the gift. And, my firstborn son, Dennis Jr., is gifted as well. But, back to Great-Aunt Maggie and the rocker.

I saw a white mist enveloping an image of Maggie as the chair rocked back and forth. Looking back, I believe that it was an energized haze of purified light. While the images in my two recounted lightning experiences were free of bodily details, not so with my departed aunt. From that day to this, her sculpted likeness, sitting in the rocker, is emblazoned in my memory.

What I saw, with clarity of vision, was a woman of middle-age. She wore a high-collared long dress and her hair was neatly wrapped in a bun. It was Maggie all right. And, I have not a single shred of lingering doubt!

I shared this experience with my cousins and only a few close relatives. Looking back with hindsight, they probably chalked it up to a young child's actively creative imagination. Nothing more. But, I assure you...I know what I saw, and the stunning memory has been securely stored away forever in the filing cabinet of my mind. And, I'm pleased to have retrieved it now so that I can share it with you.

Continuing, Rochester and Dansville are relatively close in proximity, only separated by 56 miles. So, when we left the former where I was visited by my great-aunt from the other side, we stopped in Dansville for a short visit. It was good to once again spend time with my maternal grandmother, Katherine D. McLane, and my cousin, even if the visit was intended to be abbreviated.

That night, I had a dream. I saw my grandmother, Katherine, rocking in the maroon chair that I had just seen the spirit of my Great-Aunt Maggie occupy. At the time, as a very young child, I made no sense of the message that was being delivered from a place where the word "death" has no meaning. In retrospect, the imagery is haunting—a ***premonition*** of something tragic to come! And two weeks later after returning home? We had to hastily return to Dansville because Katherine had unexpectedly died of a heart attack!

While it is unusual in contemporary times to hold a wake in a family's residence, at that time, it was a common practice in a number of very religious households. And, as a five-year-old, the fact that my grandmother's coffin occupied space in the living room parlor downstairs awaiting burial did not register as being odd in my brain. Like most children, lacking the maturity offered by experience, I accepted it as the norm.

Grandmother's coffin had been placed directly beneath the bedroom I was sleeping in. Did I, a child of little more than 60 months, understand the concept of death at the time? Probably only with a modest degree of awareness shrouded in vagueness. That's why what happened next confounded me.

Sure, Grandma Katherine's body was at rest below my bedroom; but...but...I keenly felt her presence in my room upstairs accompanied by a pervasive musty smell which I had always identified as belonging to her. Was I frightened? Strangely not because I sensed that she was conveying love to me. It's impossible to describe, but I just knew that she was surrounded by, and offering me, her love. And then my mind received a further message of comforting reassurance from her which told me that she was "at peace" and really "all right." To say I was perplexed and bewildered at the time is to understate the obvious.

"How can grandma be downstairs and upstairs at the same time?" my tiny brain yearned to know. "It must be magic," I recall saying to myself. So, what did I do? What most children of five would probably do instinctively. In the middle of night, when everyone was fast asleep, I crept downstairs to the coffin to see if grandma was still there. Well, of course she was, which toyed with my emotions and my perception of reality.

That night, shortly after falling asleep, my grandmother came to me in a *dream*. In it, and again I remember the memory as clearly as if it had been tape recorded, I heard Katherine's voice telling me: "I'm in a most beautiful place. I'm home for sure." [**Note**: Dreams can be a portal between our earthly world and a celestial realm.]

How can a child process the event I have just described? Panic? Fear? Bewilderment? Well, for me, I was composed and accepting. I felt the presence of my grandmother to be a precious gift. Why? Because I believed, no I knew, that somehow she was still with me and connected to my life. Her body had failed her, but the richness of her love endured and found refuge in my heart!

I wanted to share my experience with my family, but something or someone from **Beyond the Beyond** cautioned a child of five to conceal it from others. In looking back, I'm glad to have accommodated that voice of wisdom for surely I would have been labeled "weird" or, even worse, "crazy."

What I'm about to share with you tugs at my heartstrings and requires that I take a deep breath and wipe away more than one tear from my cheek. As I mentioned earlier, the gift, and I truly recognize it as a "healing" gift intended to bring solace to others, has its genesis for me on my mother's side of the family. And my mother, Regina, was part of an unbroken psychic chain linking one generation to another generation to yet another generation.

While I have mastered the art of being a psychic-medium and accepted the gift with a generous spirit once I grew to understand its power and purpose, my mother struggled with the notion that those residing beyond death's doorstep begged that she have a receptive ear for their words. For mom, the sense of energy, or spirits around her, sent shockwaves through her psyche. Unlike today when spirituality has opened many doorways leading to what I call "the possible," during my mother's tender years, one would have been ostracized if he or she suggested, for an instant, that he or she had been visited by one whose flesh had long ago been laid to rest.

For my mother, torment followed her throughout her life since she could not begin to comprehend why she was sensing things and hearing things that her peers were not privy to. In order to cope with what she thought to be a plaguing illness, or perhaps a curse conjured up by the biblical Devil, she turned first to her religion and then, ultimately, to a caustic elixir.

Tragically, my mom became an alcoholic and, sorrowfully, whiskey never was able to anesthetize her aching heart. As a result, the normality of our family's life was shredded. And who carried the heaviest burden wrought by my mother's lack of sobriety? Me, the eldest child!

My mother was raised a strict Irish Catholic and she greeted each Sunday as a day of celebration and, more often than not, a day of sobriety when a family could actually function as nature had intended. Attending church was not simply a driving necessity fostered by repetitive tradition. No! To Regina F. McLane-Van Praagh, it fulfilled a need as important as feeding a restless stomach. We children were sent to parochial school to perfect our faith and we accompanied our mother to mass each and every Sunday. The only one excused was our father who attended, when he wished, another church in keeping with his Episcopalian upbringing.

In the early years, I can recall attending 12:30 PM church services with my mother and my brother, Michael. As young children, we were fidgety and lacking patience during what proved to be a lengthy mass. By the time we reached the consecration, which literally means "association with the sacred," my brother and I were inclined to drift back in order to relax our backs. But, our mother would have none of what she viewed as disrespect. "Kneel up! Kneel up!" she would whisper in a voice just loud enough to gain our attention and our compliance. "Kneel up! Kneel up!" still rings in my ears like an alarm clock designed to enliven a subdued brain.

Not satisfied with our educational training at Catholic school… not sufficiently pleased with our religious exposure on Sundays at church…my mother made us sit and watch what seemed like endless movies that carried a religious theme and divine message. She was particularly drawn to the Blessed Mother Mary and, as mentioned earlier, St. Thérèse of Lisieux, "The Little Flower." But no amount of devotion and prayer could arrest the demons that haunted my mother's state of mind. The psychic gift of receiving messages and visitations from ***Beyond the Beyond*** tampered with her will to live and her only recourse was to deaden her emotions with a bottle of whiskey poured into glass after glass after glass Monday through Saturday.

So, what becomes of the family unit when a mother is an alcoholic and the breadwinner is hardly home at night because he is a stagehand for television and Broadway productions? The answer is that many of the domestic responsibilities are bequeathed to the firstborn child of the family, especially if she is a girl. And, that child was I.

I well up with painful emotions when I recall that I never had a real childhood because I never had a supportive mother. After age 10, for all intents and purposes, I was the mom with my mother frequently inebriated and my dad working what, by that time, had become two jobs. All I yearned for was to come home from school and smell dinner cooking on the stove. More times than not, that deserted task was left to me.

I couldn't bring friends home for fear that my mother was drunk and that nasty gossip back at school would spread like a wildfire gone out of control. If the truth be told, I freely admit that I was jealous of my friends who lived a "normal" life with loving and doting parents who spent quality time with them, bought them toys, and took them on adventurous vacations.

Quite often, after returning home from school, I would find that my mother was sprawled on the floor with blood gushing from her head. It was the alcohol, of course. She had consumed so much that she had lost her equilibrium. What was I to do? Times too many to count, I had to call my neighbor, Mrs. Clark, or my father, or even the police. Leaving school, I never knew what to expect once I opened the front door. It was heart-wrenching and downright terrorizing!

Let me preface my next recollection with the message that I love my siblings. One day, I came home from school and my mother was, believe it or not, sober. And, I could tell that she was excited to tell me something that she judged to be extremely important. Had she decided to stop drinking for good? That would have been more exhilarating than opening presents on Christmas Day, though presents were few in our household and our stockings received only a Clementine orange, which I loath to this day. Anyway, doing away with the liquor bottle was not on her mind or penciled onto her soon-to-do agenda. To my chagrin, she said in a message that reverberates in my ears to this very day: "I'm going to have another baby." To repeat again…I love my siblings. However, at the time, my only thought was…"How can you have another child when you can't take care of the ones you already have?"

Frequently, I was a forlorn child. And, the fact that my father would fight with my mother because of her addiction added another layer of stress upon my tiny shoulders and my impressionistic mind. How did I cope? To relieve my anxiety, I invariably raced to our backyard and climbed an apple tree to just escape from a sad and complicated reality. As an adult, I now understand the symbolism. The tree was planted deep into the ground encouraging my psyche also to try to become firmly rooted and grounded!

As time advanced, nothing really changed. My two brothers, my sister, and I had absentee parents. And yes, as the eldest, much fell upon me. I became the "Little Mommy" assigning household tasks to my siblings, overseeing their homework assignments, enforcing bedtime hours, and expressing heartfelt concern for their well-being. I had little time for personal time with friends. The only time when my emotions were rescued for a fleeting moment was on Sundays when my mother would suspend drinking to attend to God's work…church and preparing a proper family dinner to give thanks to the Lord. And Sunday proved even more glorious because our father was able to take time off from work and spend time with all of us. I felt as though I finally had a real dad and mom, just like everyone else.

But reality returned once Monday replaced Sunday. Regrettably, one-seventh of a week does not a week make. And, there are lessons here to be conveyed with an earnest heart... starting with family bonds trump everything...followed by unhealed wounds scar one's psyche for life...and, finally, forgiveness can be difficult, or sometimes nearly impossible, but lingering resentment slowly eats away at the tissue of one's heart.

I could be angry at my mother for abandoning her duties as a mother and sweeping them in my direction. But I realize that a psychic gift is a coin with two sides. It can be a joy-filled blessing or a disquieting haunting curse.

Grappling with being a psychic-medium was just too much for my mother to grasp and to grow to accept. She struggled to make sense of it, and, failing to do so, it clearly got the better of her. Sometimes a blessing when not properly understood can become as destructive as an incurable disease!

It became an exciting time in my life when the focus of my dysfunctional family paused for a fraction of a moment to channel all of its positive energy to me when I was to be confirmed in my mother's church. And, I couldn't constrain my elation for a single minute. The anticipation was building in my chest like a balloon being filled with helium; as buoyant as that object once it was released to float skyward.

Confirmation is one of the seven sacraments that sketches the religious upbringing of a dutiful Catholic. Its significance lies in the fact that according to doctrine, by receiving confirmation, one is sealed with the gift of the Holy Spirit and strengthened in one's Christian devotional faith and life.

Rising early to prepare for the ceremony, my mother insisted that the family, mother and kids, pile into the car to go to a local jewelry store so that she could buy me a gift to commemorate the celebratory occasion. Rarely did I get a present. So, this day promised to be a magical moment in my life.

We had left plenty of time to return home in order to properly dress in more formal attire for the afternoon service. Ready to leave, my brother Michael was the last to arrive running hastily to the car. What caused his delay would become all too apparent, and all too disquieting, later on.

As we approached the jewelry store, my heart skipped a beat and then another and yet another. It was a fire engine blaring its siren to alert drivers to yield the right of way. "Mom," I said. "I think our house is on fire!" And, I could see in my mind's eye firemen spraying water from their hoses all over our house. [*Precognition*?] My mother's reply was: "Stop that crazy thinking!" So, I silenced my tongue, but couldn't quell my concern.

After buying me a decorative pin in the shape of an ornate spoon, we returned home to relax and then dress for my confirmation. As we turned onto my street, black smoke billowed in the air and I knew that my *premonition* had been real, not imagined. Was I right?

Once my mother hit the brakes in front of our house, we all gasped in disbelief. A raging fire had engulfed the roof. Without thinking, remember I was an innocent child, I leapt out of the car. Because? I needed to rescue my beautiful gown that my mother had bought just for the confirmation ceremony. Before I could reach the door, a fireman luckily grabbed me and told me that I couldn't go in. When I explained the urgency, he promised to save my dress. What a hero he was in my mind.

Someone must have called my father at work for soon he showed up. With tears gushing in my eyes, I feared that all of my possessions, though they were few in number, had probably been destroyed by fire, water, and/or soot since my bedroom was upstairs below the fiery roof. "Don't cry," insisted my father. "The most important thing is that we are all safe." But, I still couldn't get my emotions settled because my confirmation promised to be the most important day in my unfolding life.

Putting the blaze out rather quickly, the firemen saved our house from total destruction. Thereafter, while it was being repaired, we stayed in a local motel for a number of weeks. And my precious dress? True to his assurance, the fireman, and his crew members, were able to put out the blaze before it had reached my closet and thus it was saved, except for one minor imperfection... its aroma!

Even though my dress smelled of smoke, I wore it with a smile adorning my face. As I look back, I can't help but chuckle because I vividly remember that kids attending the service begged me to let them smell the dress. They were intrigued by its scent and the story attached to its miraculous rescue.

The gift of the Holy Spirit that I received that day filled me with such elation that I put the fire completely out of my head. Fittingly, the bishop remarked that I was "a strong young lady who could overcome anything." And, I carry the vitality of that message with heartfelt passion to this very day.

And the cause of the fire? Remember that Michael was hurriedly running from the house to the car just before we left for the jewelry store? Well, my brother, who by this time had already well-cemented a reputation for being both rebellious and mischievous, had lit a match while horsing around and it ignited a mattress stored in a closet!

Since then, I've had countless *premonitions* that have visited my waking and sleeping hours from then until now. And *dreams*? Let me share an early one.

Our family decided to take a break from the congestion of the suburbs, leaving the stale air behind. It was a summer vacation in the Berkshire Mountains in Massachusetts that sent my twelve-year-old heart aflutter. Hiking, swimming, and camping whet my appetite for excitement like the advance of Christmas Day.

Laying my head on my pillow two nights before the engine of our car would begin to hum, I fell into a deep sleep. And then happiness was quickly wrestled away from me like a thief carrying off my precious belongings. A foreboding *dream* warned that something dreadful would happen on our trip, and the culprits were water and my right foot. And...and...while playing in a creek after we had settled in, I cut...you guessed it...my right foot on a piece of glass spoiling my fun for the entire trip. [**Note**: I will speak further about *premonitions/precognition* in a later chapter when I recall one involving the destruction of the Twin Towers on September 11, 2001.]

Advancing further in time, let me tell you about marriage and children fashioned by "love at first sight!"

While most are blessed with "soulful" mates, a privileged few are blessed with "soul" mates, a union of two hearts that beat rhythmically as one.

It was a warm summer's day in July. While most children my age were playing in the park or swimming laps in a pool or splashing in the Atlantic Ocean, I was trekking off to summer school at Flushing High School to make up for a deficiency in my English studies during my freshman year. Seated beside my girlfriend, Michelle, who also was making up for an undernourished grade, I spotted a boy on the bus who immediately caught my eye. And I said silently to myself, "I know one day we're going to be together." [**Precognition**?] Had someone from the other side whispered that message in my ear? I'll let you be the judge once I complete my story about Dennis.

Somehow, I knew that this unnamed boy and I were destined to meet again, and several bus rides later there he was again. Too shy to introduce myself, I just asked those residing **Beyond the Beyond** to keep an eye on him for me until providence brought us together.

Well, summer blended into fall and I was back in high school resuming studies during my sophomore year. The school had a liberal policy when it came to breaks between classes, which were called "open periods." The administration allowed us to leave the building to retrieve a bit of fresh air. So, during a lull in classes, several girlfriends asked if I wanted to go to the park to watch the boys play basketball. My mind didn't tell me to go; my body did. I felt as though I was being pulled towards the door. Were those dwelling in a celestial realm tampering with destiny? As I approached the court with my classmates, there he was! The boy who had captured my attention on the summer school bus. My legs grew wobbly and I nearly lost my balance—as well as my composure. Let me interrupt for a moment to mention the word "*manifestation*."

"*Manifestation*" is the act of willing something. You visualize it in your mind's eye and you capture and channel your internal energy and direct it to achieving or fulfilling your desire. For me, that was something that often occurred in my life. So, I questioned whether I had "*manifested*" meeting the young boy again. Although an answer never arrived to provide conclusive evidence one way or the other, I'd like to think that my obsession with a boy named Dennis was a "wish fulfilled."

As I and my girlfriends moved closer to the court, the boys paused their game for a moment to welcome our visit. One of the girls seemed to know most of the boys and took charge of introducing everyone. And then my pulse picked up speed like a racehorse sprinting towards the finish line. "Dennis, this is Lynn," said Rachel. It seems that she and Dennis knew one another since they lived on the same block. What a *coincidence*! Or was it? [*Note*: I will discuss the word "coincidence" later in the book.]

Well, Dennis politely came over to me and we chatted for awhile. Before returning to school to continue my classes, my heart told my mind: "You're going to marry this boy." [*Precognition*?] Was it love at first sight once I spotted him on the bus for the very first time? Soul mates to spend a lifetime together? Yes! At age fifteen, I had gleaned the answer "yes" twice expressed and I beamed with joy.

Little did I know at that very moment, Dennis had also envisioned a life spent with me. Let me share a secret. The first blush of romantic love is the purest form of perfection whose song serenades the universe!

Desperate to connect with Dennis, I hung around the basketball court after school but he was nowhere to be seen. When I felt the need to satisfy a spiritual urging during my adolescent years, I oft-times called upon my departed Aunt Maggie to provide guidance. And, when my mind set about to challenge my longing for Dennis, Aunt Maggie would say to me: "Be patient. He will come back in due time."

Days stretched into a week and my pining for Dennis escalated into intense desire. And then fate, or rather Rachel, came to the rescue. "Do you want to go to the candy store in my neighborhood?" she asked. "I think Dennis will be there." Well, little did I know that my soul- mate-to-be, Dennis, had put Rachel up to making the suggestion—wanting to see me as much as I wanted to see him. So, of course, I went, and my Mr. Right was waiting patiently for me. Like an experienced matchmaker, Rachel again re-introduced me to Dennis and then darted off to allow NATURE to work HER magic. And, SHE cleverly infused love into our two hearts. From that moment on, we became an inseparable couple for life.

One week after meeting at the candy store, Dennis and I were attending a party in the basement of Christine's house, a common friend. Timid and shy, I sat down and Dennis immediately came over and sat next to me. My heart nearly leapt out of my chest. Before I could barely form the word "hello," Dennis took my hand and slipped a small sapphire ring on my wedding finger. "What are you doing?" I said with a confluence of wonder and excitement. "I want you to go steady with me!" he exclaimed. And a kiss on his cheek delivered my answer quickly. And a return kiss on mine by Dennis sealed our commitment.

After the party ended, my Sir Galahad walked me to the city bus that would take us both back home. Just as the bus was pulling up to the curb to receive us, Dennis whispered: "I'm going to marry you." And, under a starlit night, my heart expressed the very same desire.

From that day forward, Dennis and I seriously dated and our love blossomed with all the sensual beauty of a ruby red rose. Parties and dances confirmed what everyone already knew—that there was no keeping us apart.

On a hot summer's day that bridged my junior and senior year of high school, Dennis and I were bored. So, on a lark, I asked him if he wanted to play with a Ouija board just for fun. And he said: "OK." I since realize that playing with a Ouija board is playing with fire. While the board might provide some insights into the future, it also has the power to attract *negative* energy that can be dangerously destructive. Anyone who has a board should dispose of it at once!

Anyway, I asked the Ouija board whether Dennis and I were going to get married and it answered "Yes." My follow-up inquiry centered around "when," and it spelled out the month of "August." Four years later, on August 28, we did exchange wedding vows. Then curiosity took us to Dennis' career path and it said: "Will retire as a detective in homicide." This thought never had entered Dennis' mind. Did the answer ring true? As destiny would have it, Dennis did become a New York City police detective.

Following graduation from high school, I mirrored my mother's career path at the start. Like her, I gained employment with Walt Disney Productions at their offices located in Manhattan. That lasted two years until I became pregnant. In later years to bring additional income to the family, I joined American Airlines as a manager of flight attendants.

Dennis and I were eager to get married, but he hadn't as yet "popped the question" as the expression tutors. One morning, Dennis called to tell me that he and his brother, Gary, were taking Gary's boat out of the marina in Bayside, Queens, New York, for a leisurely ride on the water. Moments after we hung up, I had a foreboding warning that coursed through my nervous system determined to arrive at my brain posthaste. [*Precognition*?] And, the psychic in me understood what was to come for three hours later Dennis called from a doctor's office. It seems that when the two brothers returned to shore, Dennis cut his foot badly when he jumped out of the boat onto the ramp landing on a piece of broken glass just waiting to put a miserable footnote, (no pun intended), to what had been a glorious day. Stitches too numerous to count closed the wound, a pair of crutches became his companion for weeks to come, and he was told to try to keep off of the foot as much as possible and to elevate his leg to aid the healing process.

A week or so passed and I was returning home from work. It was a hot and sultry summer night and I recall perspiration dripping down my cheeks. Moments from the front door, I saw the strangest sight. Dennis was parked by the curb with his foot hanging out of the window. Why? Because he was heeding the doctor's advice about elevating his foot whenever he could. Well, that was my Dennis!

"Get into the car," Dennis insisted with a voice that was showing impatience. So, I hopped into the front seat and then he said something that threw me for a *loop*. "We have to go to Greenwalds Jewelers in Flushing," he said with an eagerness that couldn't be contained.

Once we reached the jewelry store, Dennis told me to stay put. Struggling with the crutches, he awkwardly managed to reach the front door to usher himself in and then, shortly thereafter, he returned to the car trying to avoid placing his injured foot on the ground. "What's going on?" I asked with bated anticipation dying to know. Silence was his answer prompted by a smile. The next thing I knew, he was taking me home.

When we reached my house, Dennis pulled up to the curb and deadened the car's engine, and the mystery was answered. "Don't get out of the car," he insisted and, like a magician well-trained in the art of prestidigitation, he pulled a proverbial rabbit out of a hat, or, in this case, a small box from his pocket. Before a blush could color my excited face, Dennis asked: "Will you marry me?" And my response? Well, as you can guess, the rest is history.

The ring that adorned my finger had a small diamond, but the symbolism made the size much larger in my mind. We were soul mates determined by the force of the universe to be bathed in eternal love, not for a calendar lifetime but forever forged by the merger of limitless space and time!

With the approval of two sets of families, our pledge of love looked forward to a wedding that was to be held at the Sacred Heart Church with a reception to follow at Burburans Hall. Everything was falling neatly into place since Dennis had just learned that he had passed the Police Officers' test and would immediately begin his training at the academy.

As days blended into weeks, our big day was approaching with the intensity of a hurricane. Did I say hurricane? Believe it or not, days before we would exchange our vows the weather prognosticators were predicting a hurricane the day of our wedding. Yes, a full-fledged disastrous storm named "Doria." Was I worried? No! I was terrified!

The day before we were to be married, the skies turned dark… the winds began to howl…and the pitter patter of raindrops grew in volume and drenched the landscape. I remember walking to the hairdresser and saying to myself: "This time tomorrow, I'll be married. I hope and pray."

Married during a hurricane? Could it be possible? Roads saturated…guests stranded…my limousine marooned on a flooded street…flower deliveries and food caterers thrown off schedule… raging winds and rains playing havoc with hair and dress clothes. It promised to be a collective disaster of disasters for a bride waiting years for her wondrously magical day to arrive.

The night before the wedding, I can't tell you how much I focused all of my energies to send that storm out to sea. With howling winds and torrential rains beating ferociously on my windowpane, I tried to fall asleep to quiet my nerves. Tossing and turning like I was on a rocking ship on a stormy sea, I finally managed to drift into slumber land for a short while until the light of day peaked through my window.

Well, fate proved to be generous to me starting the morning of my wedding. Whether it was prayers directed to the heavens…or those exercising influence from the other side…or just damn good luck…the rain and winds had vanished and hints of blue were starting to paint the sky. Gazing out of my window in thankful relief, I spotted a flower truck stopped by our house's curb and a man, carrying a beautiful bouquet of red roses, exited the vehicle and then made long strides towards my front door.

Sent to me by Dennis hours before we were to become husband and wife, the note that accompanied his generous gesture of heartfelt affection simply read: "*I LOVE YOU*! *Love Dennis.*" It was a message that is still tucked away for safekeeping in my jewelry box at home, a constant reminder of our lifelong fidelity.

With a disaster erased from the day, our wedding went off without a hitch. It proved to be a perfect afternoon that boasted tantalizing blue skies! I couldn't have asked for a better day in the breadth of my lifetime or, for that matter, a better partner in life to share it with!

Two years after we were married, we welcomed a son into this world who was named after his doting father. Indescribable bliss caressed our hearts when little Dennis Jr. opened his eyes wide and we cradled him in our arms for the very first time. But the abiding happiness we felt was interrupted by tears when Dennis Jr. was found to be jaundiced and had to be removed to an isolation room.

"Why can't life flow easier?" I questioned aloud to Dennis, knowing the answer that: "Struggles make us stronger and encourage us to appreciate the beneficent times in our lives!" Well, our little boy finally came home and three more siblings, (Gail Lynn, Christopher Gary, and Gregory Matthew), would eventually join him to make our *house* a loving *home*. Little did we know at the time that our firstborn would be blessed with a psychic gift that he had inherited from his grandmother and mother. Now a family of six, if the truth be told, it should have been seven. Why? Between pregnancy numbers 3 and 4, I had a miscarriage. Although the gender was never determined by testing, I know that the fetus was a girl. And please, take this on faith, I feel her presence around me at times.

With a growing family—in physical size as well as in numbers—it was time to leave our Queens apartment and to find a home. At the urging of Dennis' brother Gary, we moved to Long Island less than a mile away from Gary's house. Dennis was as close to his brother as any brother could be. They not only shared a life together as police officers, they also shared the unbreakable bond of brotherly love deeply rooted in family. Sadly, misfortune intervened to sever that cord as Gary, in the springtime of his life, died tragically in a motorcycle accident. That day, I lost a dear... dear...dear brother-in-law. That day, Dennis lost a piece of his heart! Our third child, Christopher, now honors his uncle's memory with his name connected to his...Christopher Gary Gratton.

I want to move on and tell you in detail about my gift, but I'd like to take a moment to tell you about my mother's passing since it strongly influenced my path in life.

It started out as a lump in my mother's breast. In an era when medicine had not made strides to offer less invasive treatments, mastectomy was my mother's only recourse. And, she weathered the physical and emotional consequences like a trooper.

My mother banished concerns and allowed them to drift away in order to quell the anxiety voiced and felt by others. Soon, she was back on her feet, but not for long. She experienced what the doctors called a "mini-stroke" followed weeks later by a more devastating stroke which paralyzed the entire right side of her body. Tragically, she couldn't return home. Not then! Not ever! She was admitted to a rehabilitation center and then permanently transferred to a nursing home facility because she couldn't speak, walk, or control her right side. She remained there for five years until she passed through ***Eternity's Gate.***

When news arrived of my mom's passing in the home, I raced to the nursing facility. Standing by her bedside with my dad, I couldn't help but notice that she had the most amazing smile on her face. I kissed her on the cheek for one last time and softly whispered in her ear: "Mommy, you are finally at rest. You never truly understood the gift that you were given, but I do. And, I promise to use it for good to bring *love* and *peace* to those in need." Strangely, I felt her energy above us looking down and trying to still our grief. It was an amazing sensation that still gives me the chills when I glance back in time to recall the moment.

At her funeral, before her casket was closed, I saw light or energy surrounding her earthly remains. And, I closed my eyes and spoke to her telling her to journey to **Beyond the Beyond** on butterfly wings. At that moment, I vowed to honor her legacy by fully embracing her gift to me...the **healing** power that attaches to one who is a psychic-medium. And so, by helping others, I help myself to constantly refresh my memory of my mother!

For me, life has evolved, sending me on a journey of discovery as I advanced from childhood to adolescence and then into adulthood. Intuitively, I knew that I had a gift to share with others but, like a seed planted in the soil hidden from view, it took time to gather strength to pierce through a hidden veil and then fully blossom into something beautiful. I am still learning. I am still yearning to know more about myself and the reason why I was blessed with a unique gift that few are privileged to have. And, at times, quite unexpectedly, my book of life has advanced from one chapter to another chapter bringing new insights into my life. As my time on earth has lengthened, puzzle pieces, meaningless by themselves, have begun to form a coherent picture when paired with others.

It had been my belief through my early formative years that I was traveling life's path without one special voice of inspiration to guide me. Certainly, family and friends were present to offer advice, solace, and, when needed, motivational direction. But an incorporeal or ethereal energy providing what we humans call "intuition" or "wisdom" to channel decision-making never crossed my mind until a family member and I embarked upon a cruise to visit ports in Europe. Little did I know when I boarded the ship that another destination would be added to my journey; the start of a sojourn that would allow me to rendezvous with my *Spiritual Master Teacher*.

Aboard the vessel was a guest lecturer named Brian Leslie Weiss. Educated at Columbia University, and then earning a degree at the Yale University School of Medicine, Brian eventually became Head of Psychiatry at Mount Sinai Medical Center in Miami, Florida. There, employing hypnosis as a tool to aid in delving into the mind of his patients to retrieve buried information that would assist him in the healing process, he discovered something quite astonishing. While under hypnosis, a patient named "Catherine" began to relive past-life remembrances.

Dr. Weiss never seriously entertained the idea of *reincarnation* before meeting Catherine. And, quite frankly, he was taken aback when she revisited the past. Intrigued, Brian Weiss set out to validate or to invalidate her story through an exhaustive examination of the public records. To his amazement, he discovered that her memories under hypnosis were just as she had recited. From that moment forward, Dr. Brian Weiss was persuaded that *reincarnation* was fact not fiction. Since then, he has consistently found that many phobias reported by his subjects have their genesis in past-life experiences. Fear of water was caused by a prior-life drowning. Discomfort by a high-collared blouse was evidence of a past-life hanging. And, so on and so on. Thus, the experience with Catherine reshaped the doctor's ambition in life propelling a career devoted to researching "reincarnation, past-life regression, future-life progression, and survival of the human soul after death."

So, back to the European cruise. It happens that Dr. Weiss was offering a past-life regression seminar and destiny, (or perhaps my *Spiritual Master Teacher*), led me to a chair to surrender to Brian Weiss' soothing voice. And…and…in no time, I was transported back in time to what I would later learn from digging into the historical records was December 29, 1890.

In a regressive state, I clearly saw myself as a young boy,

approximately 12 years of age. I was in the American West on an Indian reservation, later learning that it was the Lakota Pine Ridge Indian Reservation in South Dakota. I was a Native American.

That past-life day, the air was thick with the stench of impending despair present as cavalry soldiers, dressed in their blue uniforms, rode swiftly onto the reservation. Why? History records to confiscate guns and rifles from the Lakota tribesmen. Experiencing the moment as vividly as though I were sitting in a movie theater watching a drama unfold, I saw the soldiers firing and killing men, women, and children. And then…and then…a bullet entered me and I was dead! Yes, I had been shot and killed. Strangely, my vision tutored that I had been mortally wounded that day, 126 years ago! How disturbing! How surreal!

Needless to say, the experience left me confused and alarmed. This was the first time that I had viewed myself living a past life, although instinctively I knew that my present life was just one of many which I will detail in chapter **FOUR**. The vision that my mind absorbed was vivid and heart-wrenching, and it took more than a moment to digest its powerful message. I am, still to this day, living with the memory seared onto my visual consciousness.

Upon reflection, I now know that the regression was intended to live with me well beyond the moment. "But why?" I questioned myself. Time would be my ally and teach that it was meant to lead me to my *Spiritual Master Teacher*!

Before moving forward, let me briefly tell you about the Wounded Knee Massacre where I died, which occurred near Wounded Knee Creek on the Lakota Pine Ridge Indian Reservation.

After the sun had barely risen on December 29, 1890, part of the 7th Cavalry Regiment led by Colonel James W. Forsyth entered the Lakota reservation to disarm the native people. A scuffle ensued with a deaf tribesman named "Black Coyote" and then, the next thing that happened, soldiers began indiscriminately firing at Lakota men, women, and children. Some Indians retreated, claimed their weapons, and began firing back. But, it was futile, for the Indians were outnumbered and outgunned. Those Lakota who managed to survive fled. However, their desperate attempt to escape proved to be in vain as cavalrymen pursued and killed them even though many carried no arms.

The dead totaled 299 Lakota and 25 soldiers. At the start, the reservation had been home to only 350 Native Americans: 230 men and 120 women and children. After the event, there were only 4 men and 47 women and children left to bury their dead and to mourn their loss.

Following the Wounded Knee Massacre, 20 cavalrymen were the recipients of the Medal of Honor. The National Congress of American Indians petitioned the American government to rescind the awards. Their pleas fell on deaf ears. Today, the battlefield has been designated a National Historic Landmark. The treatment of the American Indians is a scar on the cherished history of this country along with the treatment of Black Americans. Inhumanity is a hallmark of the chronology of history since the dawn of civilization. But, returning to Dr. Weiss' regression, it allowed me to connect to the past so that I could make sense of the future. It wouldn't be long thereafter before I was introduced to my *Spiritual Master Teacher*!

After the European cruise and the encounter with Dr. Weiss, a friend and I decided to vacation in South Dakota to see a part of the country which we felt would be scenically and historically inspiring. Oh yes…the fact that I carried the story of the Wounded Knee Massacre in my heart of hearts added weight to my decision to go. Our itinerary sketched out visits to Mount Rushmore, Custer State Park, the Wind Cave National Park, and more.

Our flight was bound for Rapid City, South Dakota, known as the "Gateway to the Black Hills," but a terrible storm diverted us to Denver for an overnight stay. Checking into a local hotel, we lamented to the reservation clerk that our plans had been abruptly altered by the weather. As it turned out, the hotel employee became animated when we mentioned that one of our scenic stops would be the site of the Wounded Knee Massacre.

The clerk then went on to tell us that she was half Native American and that her uncle, a Lakota, had been buried in a cemetery on the grounds of the Pine Ridge Reservation. After informing us of her uncle's name, the young lady asked if we would kindly "check on the grave and take a picture." How could we refuse? We couldn't and didn't!

The atmosphere cleared the next morning and, in no time, the wheels of the plane touched down in Rapid City, South Dakota. As sightseeing days blended, we eventually found ourselves at the Pine Ridge Reservation to tour the National Historic Landmark. Excusing myself, and then leaving my companion for several minutes, I was attracted to a fenced-in area, not knowing that it was the resting place of Chief Red Cloud, perhaps the most important leader of the Oglala Lakota. Slowly opening the gate, I proceeded to a bench by his grave where I seated myself to show respect and to close my eyes in contemplation. And then....

Well, let me pause for a moment to introduce you to Chief Red Cloud. The diversion is purposeful for the greatness of the man cannot be blithely overlooked.

A prominent leader of the Oglala Lakota, Red Cloud was born sometime in 1822 close to the forks of the Platte River, in close proximity to North Platte, Nebraska. He died at the age of 87 on December 10, 1909 on the Pine Ridge Reservation where he was buried.

Admired and respected for his bravery and courage, Red Cloud fought to preserve Native American lands and their diminishing cultural heritage. A fierce warrior, between 1866 and 1868, he confronted the United States Army in a campaign that came to be known as "Red Cloud's War" to defend Indian territorial rights in the Powder River Country in northeastern Wyoming and southern Montana. The Fetterman Fight or Massacre, (or the Battle of the Hundred Slain), proved to be Red Cloud's greatest triumph against the invading forces. It was the worst military defeat sustained by the U.S. Army on the Great Plains until the Battle of the Little Bighorn ten years later.

In 1868, when Red Cloud's War concluded, the Chief signed the Treaty of Fort Laramie, which fashioned the Great Sioux Reservation, and "he led his people in the important transition of reservation life." Thereafter, Red Cloud made a number of trips to Washington, D.C. to lobby for better treatment of his clansmen, meeting personally with President Ulysses S. Grant and Commissioner of Indian Affairs Ely S. Parker.

Buried on the Pine Ridge Reservation, Red Cloud was lauded as both a warrior and a diplomat trying to find common ground with the white man. Shortly before his death, he reportedly grieved:

> *They made us many promises, more than I can remember.*
> *But they kept but one—They promised to take our land…*
> *And they took it.*

The United States Postal Service honored Chief Red Cloud posthumously with a 10 cent "Great Americans" series postage stamp.

Now back to my story. Sitting on a bench in front of a renowned Native American hero, I felt a reverence that defies description. With eyes closed, I heard the crying and soulful wailing of men, women, and children. For an instant, I was unpredictably drawn back to the massacre at Wounded Knee which I had experienced during my regression with Dr. Weiss. Then, the anguishing chorus of voices subsided just as quickly as they had arrived.

I opened my eyes. The air was still, not a breeze to be felt that entire day until a whisk of wind arose from nowhere and cleansed my face. And then I felt an ***energy***, his energy, envelop me like a father embracing a child. And then…and then…I heard the timbre of his voice and these soothing words spoken with the beauty of feeling: "You are safe my child. I will always be with you and protect you into eternity and teach and guide you in this lifetime." Tears then began to stream down my cheeks and I asked the spirit or energy of the departed Chief: "Are you my ***Spiritual Master Teacher***?" And his crisp reply was a demonstrative "Yes!" No further words were spoken. No further questions were asked for there were none needed.

I sat on the bench for a few more lingering moments, but it seemed like forever. I couldn't quench my need to cry. Almost involuntarily, I rose to my feet dazed but alert. The air was quiet like it had been before I arrived. However, when I opened the gate to leave, my body was again welcomed by a gust of wind. And, I knew the source like I knew my own name…Chief Red Cloud had once again evidenced his presence by bidding me farewell.

Hysterical tears greeted my friend as we reunited. It was hard to stem the flow. It was hard to place into sentences the revelation I had encountered. "Why me?" again I asked as I have done countless times before. Because, I reasoned, I had died as a child here—on this very same Lakota Pine Ridge Indian Reservation which now holds the earthly remains of Chief Red Cloud!

I returned to New York now believing that Chief Red Cloud was indeed my ***Spiritual Master Teacher*** who would help guide and direct my life so that I could make proper use of my psychic gift. But doubt crept into my thinking and I craved further proof to rinse away any lingering uncertainty. So, two years later, I decided to return to South Dakota to visit my mentor's grave to bring finality to my mind. I begged to know with absolute certainty that Chief Red Cloud was my *Spiritual Master Teacher* and if my future years were meant to be devoted to psychic healing. And, before boarding a flight to return to his resting place, I asked him to show me a sign to bring confirming affirmation.

I did return to his gravesite with both excitement and apprehension, not knowing what to expect. But, like I always do, I felt that a message would be delivered to me by "the positive energy of the universe." When I barely reached the fenced-off area, I saw a pickup truck kicking up dust heading towards me, eventually coming to a halting stop. A woman first exited the vehicle and headed towards me and the resting place of Chief Red Cloud. Following behind her was a man who introduced himself as James Red Cloud, the great-great-grandson of Chief Red Cloud. Both had come to honor their progenitor.

When I explained who I was and the purpose for my visit, a smile greeted the face of James and, with exuberant cordiality, he invited me to follow him back to the home of Chief Oliver Red Cloud, the fourth-generation direct descendent of Chief Red Cloud, who had become Chief of the Oglala Lakota, also known as the Oglala Sioux, following the death of his father Charles Red Cloud. Was this the sign that I had hoped would greet me after trekking across the country on a pressing mission? Fate would not deny me an answer. So, I welcomed the invitation much like a child eager to be driven to an ice cream parlor.

When I shared the hospitality offered by Chief Oliver Red Cloud, I learned that he was the spiritual leader of his tribe having devoted his life to preserving the rituals and heritage of his people. Living in modest quarters, an understatement, age had taken its toll and the Chief was confined to a wheelchair. Later, I was told that his age was 91.

In the room where I was received, I noticed five pictures on the wall of Native Americans dressed in what I judged to be ceremonial attire. Instantly, my heart was drawn to one and I asked if he was Chief Red Cloud. The answer confirmed my intuition. Then, I explained my past-life regression and my visit to the Chief's gravesite two years earlier.

"Why have you returned?" questioned Oliver. "To satisfy my need to know if the great Chief is my *Spiritual Master Teacher*." Barely exhaling a breath, Chief Oliver said a simple "Yes." I was stunned by his rapid reply and then he assured me that he had spoken the truth. As to the matter of committing the remaining years of my life to that of a psychic-healer, he validated what I always had harbored in my thoughts—that I was meant to use my gift for a beneficent purpose.

Not wishing to impose and to overstay my visit, I prepared to excuse myself by expressing gratitude that was genuinely extracted from my heart. It had taken many decades, but at last I could identify a companion who was accompanying me on my life's journey to provide insightful awareness and healing to others—Chief Red Cloud! Before I reached the door, however, Chief Oliver asked me to pause for a lingering moment. Rolling his wheelchair to his bedroom and then hastily returning thereafter, he carried a smile on his face and a card in his hand which he presented to me as a lasting remembrance of my visit and as an enduring *reminder*.

The card had a colorful photograph of Chief Oliver decked out in his native ceremonial attire. "Take this," he said with unbounded delight. "It will serve to *remind* you of your spiritual connection to Chief Red Cloud and your *past* life as a Native American, a life to be honored in *this* life." And true to his message, I continue to treat the card with reverence as a treasured keepsake which bridges my past to the present as a student enrolled in the *spiritual school of learning*!

Do we all have a *Spiritual Master Teacher*? Yes, one or more;

although you may not be privileged to know his or her or their names. You are also blessed with *Earth Guides* and *Celestial Guides*, positive energies that surround our earthly being. They are that inner voice that tells us to go right not left to avoid an unseen calamity. As I mentioned earlier, some call it "intuition" or a "gut feeling," but it is a vibrating essence. While it does not make us immune from all calamities, it strives to help us lessen the dangers that are encountered as we navigate through life. They resonate with a **higher frequency of energy**.

Often I am told by a parent that his or her child claims to have an imaginary friend who he or she talks to. I'm asked: "Could this be an *Earth Guide* or *Celestial Guide*?" My answer is "most probably." There is an innocence that young children harbor that has not yet been corrupted or compromised by worldly interactions. Captured by this purity, the energy emanating from a guide is more easily harnessed by a child's incorruptibility.

I've never seen the image of one of my guides, but I have heard voices countless times. On one occasion, I asked who it was and she introduced herself to me early on and called herself "Lucy" for short, but I believe her name may be "Lucinda" or "Lucia." I've come to know that her composition is of a **higher energy** than my *Spiritual Master Teacher* and that she faithfully watches over me. She is my personal "*Guardian Protector*."

While my *Spiritual Master Teacher* is not always with me, my *Protector* is. "So," you might ask, "can I get myself into a mess even though Lucy watches over me?" Yes, indeed. Will my *Protector* do *her* best, or perhaps *its* best, to alter my misjudged course of action or misguided judgment? Yes, but the ultimate choice when a decision is meant to be made inevitably resides within me!

I also know with certitude that there are other guides that engage with us, but remain unseen. You may not be aware of their presence but, as a psychic-medium, I have encountered more than a few. When I do a reading for parents when a young child has passed, a 5-year-old "*joy*" guide named "Lulu" helps me to connect to the infant or youngster who has transitioned from the earth. Let me highlight just one of many stories.

Recently, I attended a barbecue in Upstate New York. There, I encountered a little girl who wore a pink frilly dress, white anklet socks, and black patent leather shoes. Her hair was curly and her temperament was impish. Once seen, she seemed to vanish from my sight; hiding I suspected. I described her to those present; however, no one identified with her and I quickly dispatched her from my memory until...destiny intervened to introduce me to her mother!

Once I left Upstate, I attended a metaphysical life conference in Chicago. I was a guest and not a presenter. Looking for a bite to eat, I went to the hotel's restaurant. Because of the large number of convention attendees, available seats were "as scarce as hen's teeth" as the expression goes.

Three ladies seated at a round table near the bar recognized my distress and graciously asked me to join them since there was a spare chair. They soon discovered that I was a psychic-medium because I mentioned that I saw a dapper black man in spirit standing by one of the ladies. When I described him, the stunned lady acknowledged that that was her deceased husband. She was, in her own words, "blown away."

After sitting for awhile, one of the three ladies excused herself to puff on a cigarette in the corridor outside of the restaurant. There, fate, but more than likely Lulu, intervened. The lady who was congesting her lungs with nicotine-laced smoke met a complete stranger who introduced herself as Michelle. Striking up a conversation, the lady learned that Michelle had recently lost a daughter within the past six months. Well, you probably have guessed what happened next. Michelle was escorted to my table to see if I could connect to her lost child. Time for Lulu to step in with a message from the deceased girl!

"Ask mommy to show you a picture of me," Lulu's voice echoed in my brain. And I did. And then she did. And what did the little child look like? She wore a pink frilly dress, white anklet socks, and black patent leather shoes. Her hair was curly like Shirley Temple's. She was the mysterious girl that I had encountered in Upstate New York for a fleeting moment. How incredible!

You might ask: "If I can speak to the departed, how do I avoid going crazy with departed energies constantly driving me nuts wanting to speak to a living loved one?"

I was blessed with a gift to be sure, but the challenge was learning to use it wisely and to control it effectively. There is an ominous potential for me to become unnerved as visitors from the other side compete to have their messages delivered to an ear residing on this earthly plane. Unless I learned to shut down the chatter, or, as I like to say, "pull down the curtain," my brain would otherwise be assailed like the night-bombing Blitz that pounded poor London during the summer of 1940.

Once I decided to devote myself fulltime to becoming a spiritual healer, I knew that I had to perfect my chess moves. Why? Because I was intruding upon other people's emotions. I needed to get things right much like a surgeon has to display skill lest he cause more ill than good.

Over decades, I've attended countless spiritual developmental classes, sought out those who are renowned in the field for advice and counseling, attended lectures and workshops, and read and read and read. I am privileged to have many friends in the spiritual healing world.

With confidence building, I began doing personal readings, slowly at first but eventually gaining momentum. As I changed lives with positive messages from the other side, my confidence and self-worth grew. I was given a gift, and I'm proud to say that I did not squander the opportunity to become an emissary channeling hope and peace to those suffering from troubling despair. As my skills blossomed from one reading to the next, abetted by research and by attending seminars and workshops, individual readings became group readings and then I was enlisted to mentor spiritual development classes throughout the United States. And now? I've garnered sufficient knowledge and wisdom worthy to share with countless strangers struggling for answers. So, to answer the preceding question, I've disciplined myself to "pull down the curtain" and to shut out all of the noise from the place where death is unknown until I need to reach out to departed energies.

How has being a psychic-medium changed my life you might ask? Capturing but one word, I would say…"*empathy*!" I care about people like a social worker devoting his or her life trying to arrest the suffering and hopelessness of others. There is nothing on this plane of existence more traumatic than losing a loved one—a spouse, a child, a sibling, a grandparent, a special aunt or uncle, a best friend, or a person who transformed your life with a bounty of love and encouragement. Losing touch is like losing a limb. You challenge yourself to move forward and to cope with a heartbreaking loss. "If only they weren't truly gone *forever*!" you lament with tears in your eyes. Well, the good news is that they are not gone *forever* and, thanks to my gift, I, and others, can channel their messages to provide hope and expectation…the expectation that one day you will surrender your bodily flesh and your true "*life force*" or *energy* will soar to reunite with them and their enduring energy. So, to end the long version of my life story, you might ask: "How has my gift changed my life?" It has made me humble and grateful. Humble that I was blessed with a unique gift that can stitch a broken heart back together. Grateful that I can wipe away a tear and produce a lingering smile!

Before I end this brief biographical journey, let me conclude by reflecting upon the life and death of my husband, Dennis, and the legacy he entrusted to our children.

Service! There is no greater gift that one can give to his fellow man than to pursue a career that puts others above self! And, that was my Dennis' ambition having settled in his mind and heart at a very tender age.

Assigned to the 28th Precinct in Harlem, New York, Dennis proudly donned the uniform of a New York City patrolman wearing shield #5000, a powerful number that evoked strength and confidence in the man who wore it. Lessons learned on the streets of a vibrant and, at times, violent city, Dennis proved his worth facing countless challenges head-on displaying courage and compassion. In time, he surrendered his badge for one that read #3599 honoring a promotion to detective. He would serve for 20 years as a protector of the peace, retiring at age 39. His best friend and partner, Ray, was sad to see him leave the force but understood the reason for a sudden departure at such an early age when more years could have been added to his pension.

It was a traumatic event which catapulted Dennis into making a decisive heart-wrenching decision. Responding to a call, Dennis' will to continue on as a detective was crushed when he saw a two-year-old girl robbed of life with a hanger wantonly wrapped around her neck. Who was the perpetrator of such a despicable act of inhumanity? A mother on drugs!

While some police officers are somehow able to anesthetize their emotions when witnessing a crime scene, Dennis couldn't suppress his feelings, particularly when children were helpless victims of abuse or regrettably far worse. Thus, he abbreviated his first love for a second after receiving numerous commendations and medals for bravery and service to the community.

Joining his father-in-laws' profession, and with his help and guiding hand, Dennis was hired as a Broadway stagehand and joined Local #1 of the I.A.T.S.E. He became what in the trade was called a "flyman," bringing in a continuing change of scenery to compliment an unfolding story. There were many exciting performances that he carried home to share with our family. Perhaps the most memorable was the original *Grease* production starring John Travolta. Later, Dennis persuaded our son, Dennis Jr., to join him as a flyman and they worked together…Dennis controlling the scenery on the left-hand side of the stage and Dennis Jr. on the right.

June 7, 2000 was the last day we all got to share with Dennis… for his life ended and an ocean of tears were shed which emptied more than one tissue box. He was only 48.

His last show was the memorable 1999 Broadway revival of *Kiss Me, Kate*, a musical version of Shakespeare's *The Taming of the Shrew* with music and lyrics composed by Cole Porter and performed at the Martin Beck Theater, later renamed the Al Hirschfeld Theater in 2003. As a tribute to Dennis, the theater was darkened and a moment of silence was requested from the audience to honor his sudden passing.

My Dennis was a skeptic when it came to my calling. However, we mutually agreed that whoever passed first would leave a ***dime*** for the survivor to find in order to acknowledge that he/she had safely transitioned to the other side of death to be welcomed by ***eternal light*** and ***love***! And, true to our pledge, two weeks after Dennis' passing, something bizarre happened. When I awoke from bed in the morning, a ***dime*** had deposited itself by my right thigh. And a verifying message came to me in a ***dream*** shortly thereafter when I heard Dennis' voice, clear and filled with regrets, apologizing to me and our four children "for leaving so soon." With candor, I tell you that I often feel an energy presence around me and I know that it's my beloved Dennis watching over me to offer protection and guidance.

As a psychic-medium, my connection to ***Beyond the Beyond*** has allowed me to process Dennis' passing in a way that others cannot. I know that when Dennis entered ***Eternity's Gate*** he was received by his brother, Gary, and his paternal grandmother, Edith. Since human existence is "timeless," I know that by destiny's design I will one day be reunited with my soul mate.

Before celebrating Dennis' legacy in the next section, our four wonderful children, let me add these postscripts about my significant other. Dennis loved baseball and his New York Yankees. Attending a game with his father at age 8, Dennis had the rare privilege of catching a foul ball. Somehow, his father prevailed upon management to get Yogi Berra and Roger Maris to sign what became a treasured keepsake. Later, his attachment to the Yankees became even more pronounced when, as a police officer, he would be assigned to a security unit to patrol the stadium. Meeting countless players…most notably, Thurman Munson and Billy Martin…Dennis shared many stories with us about the heroes who wore the pinstripes.

Dennis loved music and tried his hand at playing the guitar. His favorite group was by far the Beatles, collecting records and playing and singing their songs like the most admiring Beatlemania fan. His fondest memory of the "Fab Four" was when he attended their 1964 concert at the old Shea Stadium. I'm sure that that became ingrained in his memory as vividly as our very first date.

Dennis was also athletic. He was a bowler and even recorded a perfect 300 game. Also, he was on a NYCPD softball team and loved the camaraderie and competition.

I could fill page after page recounting the depth of my love for Dennis but simply stated—*He was my soul mate*! Although I am now one-half of what used to be a whole, I feel at peace. Why? Because with each breath that I take, I know that on some meant-to-be tomorrow we will once again be joined to become ***one***.

My biographical visit would be incomplete without paying homage to a marriage that welcomed four beautiful and gifted children into our lives. Attributed to a minister named Lyman Abbott, this partial quote resonates with me:

A child is a beam of sunlight from the Infinite and Eternal….

Thus, let me briefly introduce the beams of sunlight that graced Dennis' and my life.

(1) ***Dennis Jr.:***

Named after his father with a suffix attached to honor his father's legacy, Dennis Jr., as mentioned earlier, works as a Broadway stagehand and his résumé also includes working at NBC at 30 Rockefeller Plaza. He is a member of Local #1 of the I.A.T.S.E.

Gifted musically, playing both the piano by ear and a bass guitar, the latter being a 67 Fender that was cherished by his father, I am proud to share the fact that Dennis Jr. has inherited a level of spirituality that is quite unique. He is a "sound healer," using his musical talents to bring comfort to others.

Our son has appeared on stage with me. Picking up the frequency of one who has passed and who is connected to a person in the audience, Dennis Jr. composes spontaneous musical notes that are miraculously woven together to produce a healing melody. At the same time, I am able to tune my vibrational frequency to receive a message from the other side and to convey it to the seated person paired to the music. It is simply amazing and beyond my powers of explanation.

(2) ***Gail Lynn***:

Happily married with three glorious children, Gail has acquired a different spiritual gift. She is a Reiki healer. As a Reiki practitioner, Gail uses a technique called "hands-on healing" through which a "universal energy" is transferred through the palms of her hands to one suffering emotional or physical pain to bring relief. She is working hard to elevate her healing powers.

Additionally, Gail has found a deeper level of spirituality through meditation and the use of crystals. She now has an on-line business to introduce others to the healing power of crystal quartz stones.

(3) ***Christopher Gary***:

Happily married with two glorious children, Chris has followed what has become a family stagehand tradition. He works at the Jones Beach Theater on Long Island, is a stagehand for Broadway productions and for *SNL,* and *30 Rock,* when it ran, and is a member of Local #1 of the I.A.T.S.E. Additionally, he has his own electrical business. An ambitious hard worker, so far a psychic gift has not shown up on his doorstep. Will it eventually come? We'll have to be patient and see.

(4) ***Gregory Matthew***:

With two glorious children, Gregg is an iron worker. He, and those who have come before him, have prided themselves on helping to build this great country with hands that are often callused and with hearts that swell with the satisfaction delivered by enduring accomplishment. He is proud to count himself as a member of Local #580 of the Iron Workers' Union. Psychic? Not as of this writing.

Dennis and I raised four beautiful children together. Each, in his or her own way, made us proud to be a giving and caring family unit of six. We weren't rich when measured in dollars, but our wealth proved to be enormous when calculated by an unending expression of love for one another. To honor the memory of a doting father and beloved husband, the five of us carry a small detective shield accompanied by a photo of Dennis.

To conclude, allow me the privilege of boasting that I have seven beautiful grandchildren who bring a bounty of joy to my life and close by briefly paying tribute to the passing of my father.

My dad, Allan, left us in 2005, at age 83, succumbing to pneumonia. By his bedside in the hospital, we all gathered to bid farewell and to pay homage to a man who captured the American spirit of hard work and love of country and family. Whispering in his ear, I said: "It's OK to go. Mommy is waiting for you." And moments later, his blood pressure dropped and he peacefully passed.

My father would always chide me by saying: "Being a stagehand is not for women." Nonetheless, two years after he left us, I interviewed with Local 1 of the I.A.T.S.E. and gained employment as an assistant to the treasurer, working for six years until I became a fulltime psychic-medium. When I arrived to apply for the job, there was a song playing in the background. Was it a sign of approval sent to me by my father from **Beyond the Beyond**? I'll let you be the judge. The song was: "Dance With My Father" sung by Luther Vandross.

THREE
What It Means To Live.

"The only reason to live is to love and the only reason to love is to live."
Tonya Hurley

What does it mean to live? In the "nunnery scene" of William Shakespeare's play *Hamlet,* Prince Hamlet, in the opening soliloquy in Act III, Scene I, stares into a self-imagined reflective mirror and profoundly asks: "To be, or not to be, that is the question;" pondering why he should live a moment longer. My answer repeats, *in part*, the chapter heading: "The only reason to live is to love and the only reason to love is to live," and this message resonated with the tragic fate of Shakespeare's star-crossed lovers Romeo and Juliet. Believing that Juliet was dead, her lover drinks poison. Believing that Romeo was dead, she stabs herself with his dagger to be united in death.

We are born seemingly with a blank slate and by our own hands and deeds we fill in the details that are meant to chronicle our lives. And, as the curtain closes, and our life draws to its ending, we wonder what lies ahead. In Hamlet's words: "...the undiscovered country, from whose borne, no traveller returns...." Well, it is my intent to fill in Hamlet's blanks for the realm he refers to is not "undiscovered" and travelers, when required, do "return."

To expand upon the theme of "what it means to live," I am reminded of the thoughts of my dear friend and collaborator, Brett Stephan Bass—attorney, businessman, world traveler, and scholar. Brett has asked himself the "living" question and discovered four reasons which I find value in sharing with you:

(1) To find your soul mate.
(2) To search for knowledge and acquire wisdom.
(3) To consider what it means, as a conscious being, to experience life.
(4) To find a deeper level of spirituality.

SOUL MATE

For me, I found my soul mate when I met Dennis. It was instantaneous, and our emotions connected like a puzzle that required only two pieces. It was a feeling that transcended mere attraction to occupy a place reserved for us where our embrace would be eternal. It was quintessential in its perfection. Why? Because it was authored and gifted by the **Source**. When I have learned all that needs to be learned on this earthly plane during this life and the next, I know that Dennis' energy will be waiting for me bathed in *love* and *light* emanating from the **Source**.

KNOWLEDGE

Kofi Atta Annan, the seventh Secretary-General of the United Nations, said:

> *Knowledge is power.*
> *Information is liberating.*
> *Education is the premise of progress,*
> *in every society, in every family.*

Never stop reading…never stop questioning…never stop challenging yourself to know more. And, hopefully, wisdom will gift itself to you!

There is so much to learn…to absorb…to file away in your brain for later use. Pick up a book on Renaissance art and immerse yourself in the beauty of Venus' face painted by Sandro Botticelli. Pick up a book on astronomy and see a universe filled with more stars than there are individual grains of sand forming every beach and every desert dotting our planet. Pick up a book of poetry and be tantalized by the use of language as it transports your mind and emotions to a newly awakened reality. Knowledge will feed your imagination. Your imagination will intensify your conscious energy and allow you to see the world not as it is but as it was meant to be!

EXPERIENCING LIFE

My father's favorite quote drew profound meaning from *Meditation XVII*. In it, John Donne, the metaphysical English poet and cleric in the Church of England, famously wrote:

> *All mankind is of one author, and is one volume; when one man dies, one chapter is not torn out of the book, but translated into a better language; and every chapter must be so translated....As therefore the bell that rings to a sermon, calls not upon the preacher only, but upon the congregation to come: so this bell calls us all....No man is an island, entire of itself...any man's death diminishes me, because I am involved in mankind; and therefore never send to know for whom the bell tolls; it tolls for thee.*

What is Donne telling us? Clearly that you and I and our neighbors across the street and around the globe are not isolated from one another. Rather, we are all interconnected. Some have called it "collective consciousness"...a "universal mind"... "universal consciousness"...and some in physics have labeled it "non-local consciousness."

What does my work as a psychic-medium inform me? That we each are connected to the universal "*oneness*" of the **Source** waiting for that moment in eternity's window when we can each reconnect to eternal **light**, **love**, and **wisdom**.

We are **one** family, all attending "*the school of earth vibrations*," sent on a journey of discovery here on mother Earth so that we can elevate our energy or vibrational frequency levels to align ourselves with the **Source**. How can we elevate our energy levels? The principal way is through **LOVE**!

Mark 12:31 says: "Thou shalt love thy neighbour as thyself. There is none other commandment greater than these."

Experiencing life means "opening one's eyes" to not only the bountiful joys of living but also to understanding suffering because the world counts more people (and creatures) in pain than those enjoying pleasure. Starvation…lack of clean drinking water… homelessness …sexual abuse…insufficient medical care are not the exception on this planet. As you advance from one day to the next, try to make a difference in a stranger's life. How? Through a caring word or a generous gesture. Why? Because, to quote Donne again: "All mankind is…of one volume." And take to heart these words spoken by Mother Teresa:

> *The greatest disease in the West today is not TB or leprosy; it is being unwanted, unloved, and uncared for. We can cure physical diseases with medicine, but the only cure for loneliness is love. There are many in the world who are dying for a piece of bread but there are many more dying for a little love.*

SPIRITUALITY

Don't look to any one religion for answers! Don't look to any one philosopher for answers! Don't look to any one scientist for answers! Because the answer to life's meaning resides within your metaphysical heart. Mother Teresa said: "The poverty in the West is a different kind of poverty—it is not only a poverty of loneliness but also of spirituality."

John Lennon once wrote:

> *I believe in God, but not as one thing, not as an old man in the sky. I believe that what people call God is something in all of us. I believe that what Jesus and Mohammed and Buddha and all the rest said was right. It's just that the translations have gone wrong.*

In the work that I have done for well over four decades, I have come to realize that there is a deeper level of understanding about the universe than mankind has grasped through the teachings of religions, science, and philosophy. I speak with the departed almost every day in healing sessions and they have imparted a valuable message..."Death is not an ending, but rather a beginning of a journey home to where the *Source* resides." Thus, life on earth prepares us for our destiny...to become "*one*" with the *Source* to truly experience the perfection of *love*.

To those who are religious...to those of you who are not...I say, be "open-minded." Allow your spiritual energy to soar...through acts of kindness...by being sensitive to the feelings of others... by releasing negative emotions allowing them to evaporate...by exploring the beauty of nature...by suppressing an ego that may be driven by materiality.

One day you will arrive at *Eternity's Gate* to be welcomed into a domain which I call *Beyond the Beyond*. What you now make of your life here on earth will determine whether your stay will be eternal...or will be brief so that you can be sent back to earth to learn one or more life lessons that will endow your *frequency* with greater *vibrational energy*!

FOUR
What It Means To Die.

"The day which we fear as our last is but the birthday of eternity."

Lucius Annaeus Seneca

Written in 1609, *Death Be Not Proud* is a fourteen-line poem penned by John Donne (1572-1631) as one of nineteen sonnets that comprise his *Divine Meditations* or *Holy Sonnets*. What I find attractive are the first two and last two lines of the sonnet:

> *Death be not proud, though some have called thee*
> *Mighty and dreadful, for, thou are not so....*
>
> *One short sleepe past, wee wake eternally,*
> *And death shall be no more; Death, thou shalt die.*

The evening before I am scheduled do a reading, I follow a traditional ritual to invite in *positive* energy. I guide myself to a spiritual place in my home where I light a candle and bathe the room in soft soothing background music. I seat myself in a comfortably cushioned chair, close my eyes, quiet my emotions, and begin a period of intense meditation intended to last approximately fifteen minutes. In no time, my mind is transported to an imaginary garden embroidered with the most colorful flowers of varying vibrant hues. The vision that I experience rivals the intensity of an artist's glorious depiction of the Garden of Eden.

Now inspired by the quietude inherent in sublime beauty, I am led to a dazzling crystal bench where I wait for my gatekeeper to usher in those with *positive* energy who are meant to join the reading the following day. And, disappointment never comes because the visitor to my consciousness oft-times carries a message from **Beyond the Beyond** to be shared with loved ones the next day.

It is easy to be dismissive. It is easy to be skeptical. Many who attend my lectures or my group or individual readings come as cynics and disbelievers. I can read it on a face or sense it when my eyes connect with body language which expresses doubt. But, being dubious is healthy. We should all be Missourians and adopt the motto…"Show Me."

I get goose bumps when the face of a *Doubting Thomas* converts from a frown into a smile. When words channeled from beyond the life-death boundary find resonating meaning to persuade a listener that those who have passed have elevated their energies to reside in a higher unseen realm of existence. I can ask: "Who passed who identified with a red carnation? Who loved to skinny-dip in a lake in the dead of night? Who played the harp? Who died accidentally on an icy road making a sharp turn and then hitting a tree? Who died of a lingering disease after returning from a trip to Europe? Who wore a ring with a hidden inscription? Who had a tattoo of the ace of hearts on her thigh? Who was a train engineer? Who collected Canadian stamps? Who was allergic to cats?" On...and on...and on...and on. Cryptic messages arrive on my lips to be shared—to honor the memory and to acknowledge the presence of one who has been liberated from his or her flesh to reside where the word "death" is meaningless—returning to earth for a brief moment to assure loved ones that life carries on beyond the grave. To, in Donne's words, to "wake eternally" and to declare that death "shalt die."

My understanding of bodily death is that our ***energy*** (or ***consciousness***) escapes and is transported on a beam of illuminating ***light*** to ***Eternity's Gate*** where we will be welcomed into an astral energy realm which I've come to know as ***Beyond the Beyond***. Here, we will be met by someone who has passed who was near and dear to us.

Coinciding with our arrival, we will immediately experience a "*life review.*" With time barely elapsing, we will **see** and **feel** every moment of our most recent life on earth like a flashback in a movie. If we brought pain to others, that pain will be experienced tenfold. If we shared joy with others, that bliss will be magnified to produce boundless elation.

If our energy is weak and malnourished, then we may be returned to earth to learn one or more life lessons as a ***reincarnated*** being. Once our ***energy, frequency,*** or ***consciousness*** has achieved a higher threshold, we remain in **Beyond the Beyond** to work to increase our energy levels to prepare for one final journey…to become *"one"* with the **Source**.

There is something about Jainism, an ancient Indian religion, that resonates with my thinking as expressed in this chapter, and the one preceding it, which is worthy of sharing with you. While no one religion is the "true" religion, each has a message that seeks to transport the mind and the heart to a place where wisdom resides. So, let me introduce you briefly to Jainism.

The word "Jain" finds its genesis in the Sanskrit word *jina*, meaning "victor" which religious scholars have interpreted as "connoting the path of victory in crossing over life's stream of rebirths through an ethical and spiritual life." The motto of Jainism is *Parasparopagraho Jivānā* translated as "the function of souls is to help one another." And, I have found that once a person's energy takes up residence on the other side, they are invested with the task of helping those left behind on earth by making their presence known through *dimes* left to be found, by messages inserted into *dreams*, and by guidance deposited into *subconscious minds*.

In Jainism, there is no God which is credited with creation. This mirrors my understanding of the eternal energy which I refer to as the **Source**. Additionally, the followers of Jainism believe that existence dispenses with the word "time," having neither a beginning nor an ending. This also pairs comfortably with my work as a psychic-medium. And, like I said in Chapter One—"mind-energy is able to survive without the need of a physical body"—Jainism creates the same dualistic reference when it speaks of *jiva* ("self" or "soul") and *ajiva* ("matter"). Later, René Descartes, (1596-1650), French scientist, mathematician, and philosopher, would champion Cartesian dualism which viewed mind and body as divisible.

Jiva, or what I call "human consciousness," is described as being eternal but imperfect, reborn again and again until it evolves to achieve "omniscience and eternal bliss," what I call being *"one"* with the **Source** of *love*, *knowledge*, and *wisdom*. Thus, Jainism reiterates my belief in **reincarnation** or the continuing cycles of rebirths and re-deaths with a designed purpose. To put an exclamation point on this bold, and, to some, incredulous statement, let me personalize the concept of **reincarnation** as I retrieve memories once woven into time.

Why are you here on this earthly plane of existence? By chance? By choice? Are the people joined in your circle of love or outer circle of friendship here with you by chance or by choice as well?

Conception occurs when a gamete, a haploid cell, fuses with another haploid cell during a process called fertilization. In humans, as with other species, the larger type of gamete, called an egg or ovum in a female, combines with a smaller tadpole-like gamete, a sperm produced by a male, to create what we have come to call a "life"…or perhaps better described as a **life energy**.

In a gambling casino, when you place a bet on a single number on the roulette wheel what are the odds that you will become a winner? Answer…35-to-1 or a paltry 2.63%! What do you think the statistical probability is that a particular sperm will find an ovum to produce what will become the uniqueness of you? Staggering when first considered; or is it?

Being a psychic-medium has taught me that your birth was not inspired by an architect of chance. It was no toss of the dice or a random shuffle of a card deck. No! You are here for a reason; a purposeful reason! And those around you? No odd coincidence authored by serendipity.

The concept of **reincarnation** has formed the backbone of many cultural belief systems and, from personal experience which I will shortly detail, it is the nutrient that feeds and shapes our energy that will allow us to eventually become "**one**" with the **Source**. Repeating the question which I posed earlier—namely, why are you here on this earthly realm of existence with family and friends?

By chance? By choice? The answer is by choice! Whether you realize it or not, you are here because you "chose" to be here and "chose" the people (or energies) who bring you comfort, joy, and sometimes grief and pain—all designed as a learning curve to help you to complete *the circle of your earthly education*.

On the other side, you have metaphorically signed a *divine contract* to return to terrestrial earth to learn one or more life lessons intended to perfect your *energy* or *eternal frequency*. And I did the same on this repeat visit having been here several times before. And, instinctively, I know that my earthly journey will continue at least one more time *hereafter* once I visit the *hereafter* when destiny calls.

Earlier, I told you that I was a young Indian boy killed by soldiers in a bloody massacre at the hands of soldiers who were deprived of a conscience. But, this was not my only encounter with a past life experience retrieved from another yesterday. There were others which I'd like to share with you to invigorate you understanding of *reincarnation* and how it plays a pivotal role in the enhancement of what religions have called an "immortal soul" or what I choose to call an *eternal energy* or *eternal frequency*.

Reincarnation

REINCARANTED TO BECOME A YOUNG GIRL LIVING IN ANCIENT TIMES

One of my dearest friends is named Ed who lives a little more than an hour north of New York City in a bucolic retreat boasting a serene tree-laden landscape and a lake that inspires tranquility. Ed is a sound engineer working for Saturday Night Live and we met a number of years ago as a result of our mutual association with Local #1 of the I.A.T.S.E.

Since meeting, I have grown to love Ed like an adopted brother feeling an instant connection during our initial introduction. As explained in the next recaptured reincarnation story, you will learn that we shared another life experience together which perhaps explains our caring closeness in this lifetime.

Know that Ed enjoys experimenting with essential oils. He says that they enhance his "energy vibrations." As for me, this is something that I never considered or tried until....

"Apply myrrh to your third spiritual eye and throat," Ed insisted two years ago at his home. "It will boost your spiritual ability to see and to speak."

[Note: Myrrh is a resin extracted from certain thorny trees that for countless centuries have been used as a medicine, perfume, or incense. In the Hebrew bible there are numerous references to myrrh. In Exodus 30:23-25, it is reported that Moses spent 500 shekels to purchase liquid myrrh to use as the main ingredient to produce sacred anointing oil. And, in the New Testament, the magi presented three gifts to the Christ Child, one being myrrh along with frankincense and gold.]

So, on a lark, I followed Ed's encouragement and applied the myrrh to my "third spiritual eye" and my "throat."

Bowing my head while closing my eyes, in no time, I felt an energy building up inside my body and I suddenly experienced a strange sensation. Inexplicably, I sensed that my life had been divided into two, marrying the present with the past— being in two places at one time! And then a movie began to unfold in my mind, (captured by my "third spiritual eye?"), and I narrated the scenes to Ed through my throat which had been dampened with myrrh.

"I've returned to ancient times," I voiced aloud. "I'm a young girl of 16 years.

I'm wearing a brown cloth garment aged by use and exposure to the sun. There are sandals on my feet and the ground is covered with dirt. I hear the chatter of voices bargaining and bartering. It's a marketplace where I find myself.

Why? Because I am selling oils at my father's insistence while he waits at home.

"Suddenly, merchants are screaming at me. Verbally berating me because the oils I'm trying to sell are said to be 'impure.' Humiliated and frightened, I race home clutching only a few coins in my right hand when my father expected many more.

"I reach my home and hand the coins to my father, explaining that the oils were 'impure.' He grows angry with me and goes into a fitful rage. He tells me to go to the seller and complain about the quality. When I tell my father that I'm afraid of the man, my father beats me. Then, I'm forced to obey.

"Confronting the seller, the man grows angry and begins to chase me. Running to save my life, I head for what appears to be a shed-like structure. Before I reach it, however, I'm enveloped by a dark mist. The story ends."

Opening my eyes and raising my head, Ed and I instantly realized that somehow I had been transported back in time to relive the tragic ending to a prior life. In my mind, the "black mist" symbolized my death! I have never used myrrh again!

Before moving on to the next reincarnation recounting, let me briefly explain what a "third eye" or "mind's eye" or "inner eye" is.

[In a number of spiritual traditions, the third eye refers to the brow chakra, a gateway to higher consciousness or enlightenment, located around the middle of the forehead. It is often linked with "religious visions, clairvoyance, the ability to observe chakras and auras,

precognition, and out-of-body experiences."
In Theosophy mysticism, it is taught that it
is associated with the pineal gland, a small
endocrine gland in the brain that produces
melatonin which modulates sleep patterns.
Believers assert that the gland is a hyper-di-
mensional gateway which allows the mind to
open a pathway that invites more profound insights to arrive which are intended to elevate
our spiritual understanding of the cosmos.]

REINCARANTED TO BECOME
A ROMAN WOMAN OF PRIVILEGE

Once we are reborn to live yet another "life of learning," we most often will share it with others from a past life who accompany us on a continuing journey to elevate our spiritual energy or frequency. Thus, it wasn't surprising to me when my beloved friend Ed, who I mentioned before, appeared in a vision that visited my "third eye" several years ago.

One day, with my eyes closed and while my mind was at ease, I was transported back in time. Was I asleep in a dream-like state? No. I simply cleansed my thoughts and a vision arrived as clear as the objects in the room when I eventually opened my eyes.

I saw flat-soled leather sandals worn by both me and a man I knew to be Ed. I believe that I was a patrician woman, a citizen-aristocrat, living in a ruling class home. I thought that I was wearing a Roman toga until later I discovered it was a stola, a traditional garment worn by Roman women like the one adorning the Statue of Liberty in New York City's harbor. It seems that after the 2nd century BCE, the toga was worn exclusively by men and that if a woman wore one it suggested that her profession was that of a prostitute.

In my vision, Ed was wearing what appeared to be Roman attire more formal than the typical toga. The details of its design now have escaped my memory. Ed and I were married with a daughter whose age was five, a number that has become reinforced in my memory. What I saw next was as alarming as the previous story I shared with you.

In an open space with a roof supported by pillars, Ed, I, and our child became frightened when we saw that a blazing fire in the distance was fast approaching our home, which seemed to me to be a mansion. Ed suddenly left us for a moment to have a closer look when he realized that it was about to engulf our home. Running back to protect us, there was little he could do. First our child died...then I died...and finally Ed was consumed by the flames.

Overcome by penetrating fright, I opened my eyes wide and immediately returned to present time. What I had captured in my mind's eye was real, and not imagined, leaving chills running down my spine!

[Postscript: In doing research, I think that my regression brought me back to the Great Fire of Rome (July 18-19, 64 CE) when countless mansions, residences, and temples were destroyed during a seven-day period. Some ancient historians blamed Emperor Nero for starting the conflagration.]

Allow me to leave you with one final reincarnation episode which transported me to a time not too long ago.

REINCARANTED TO BECOME AN ENGLISH NURSE

I was a Flight Attendant Manager for American Airlines and my responsibilities carried me to London twice a month. On one occasion, I was on a tour bus and we passed an abandoned cement building by the Tower Bridge which tugged at my energy. (Déjà-vu?) I could actually feel myself being pulled in the direction of the building and I reacted by instantly closing my eyes and an inner vision revealed the following.

"This had been a hospital," a voiced whispered to me, "and you were a nurse with 26 other nurses tending to children." Then, to offer confirmation, I was shown myself wearing a uniform which I later described as looking like the one worn in a picture I have seen of Florence Nightingale, (1820-1910), an English social reformer who founded modern-day nursing. Finally, I was shown that the hospital had been bombed, which I subsequently surmised must have occurred during World War II. I and countless others perished resulting from a violent explosion.

When I opened my eyes, we were streets away from the deserted structure and I gave it no further thought until two years later when I once again passed the same building and this time my eyes strained to search for a name on the building. And the name which was barely visible? "Children's Hospital" of London. Meaning? My momentary return to the past was confirmed by evidence which survived to reside in the present!

Did you notice something repetitive in my reincarnation stories? Did you observe the presence of a recurring theme? I didn't celebrate the beginning of life...the joys retrieved and then retold from adolescence...the challenges or successes experienced during adulthood... or the preserved memories shared with family and friends as life was slipping away in old age. No! Only the moments of death were recalled! My death as a young Native American detailed in my biographical story in Chapter Two. And here, my recounted death as a young girl in ancient times. My death as a Roman patrician woman. My death as a wartime nurse. Why only death? I strain my mind to know and strive to provide you with a possible answer.

Death is a dramatic and defining moment in one's life. It completes an expedition of exploration. Spiritually, it closes one door and allows another to open, inviting us to continue a voyage of self-discovery, self-learning, and self-purification to increase our energy frequencies so that one day we will be prepared to take up permanent residence Beyond the Beyond.

We are creatures who have eternal conscious energy that resides in bodies that are, at most, temporary sanctuaries to be discarded and then replaced until we have gained "spiritual purity." You, my reader, are here on earth to learn one or more life lessons so that a return visit will no longer be needed and your jiva ("self" or "soul") can continue its journey where all-knowing wisdom and everlasting love awaits offering an eternal embrace.

FIVE
Stories Recounted From This Side Of Life.

"A story communicates fear, hope, and anxiety, and because we can feel it, we get the moral not just as a concept, but as a teaching of our hearts. That's the power of story."
⌐ Marshall Ganz

Once word surfaced that I was considering writing a biography, I was besieged by clients and Facebook followers who begged me to recount many of my memorable readings that connected those who resided on each side of the life-death divide. Inspired to do so, this chapter, as well as the one which follows, will allow me to share a number of recent channeling sessions which have left a lasting imprint upon my mind's memory. Before I begin, however, let me advance a preface designed to gain the trust of those who approach this subject matter evincing a healthy skepticism.

What I'm about to share with you in the coming pages are events based purely upon fact and not woven out of fiction. I know that it is far too easy to use embellishment to heighten a story's dramatic punch…the product of a creative imagination. Also, it is far too easy to manufacture details intended to tamper with a reader's vulnerable believability. And I know that it is far too easy to allow a swollen ego to get in the way of candid truth-telling. With this made clear, let me tell you categorically that I will never brook deception. Why? Because I value my gift of psychic healing as divinely inspired and I know within my heart of hearts that to misuse it will have "eternal" consequences too grievous to consider.

As my pen engages with paper, I desperately want you to cast all doubts aside and accept my stories as credible. For some, this may be hard given cultural and religious prejudices. But, I beg that you be open-minded whatever your spiritual or non-spiritual grounding may be. And to help you to navigate the path of believ-ability, I would like to introduce you to a skeptic turned believer, my friend and literary collaborator, Brett Stephan Bass.

On October 10, 2015, I was invited to a private home in Patchogue, Long Island, New York, to conduct a spiritual group reading for ten invited guests. Before I set out from home, my energy levels were elevated and receptive. And, an inner voice told me something quite extraordinary. It said: "You will meet someone at the reading that destiny has willed you to befriend." Sending back two inquisitive words to the author of the message…"Who?

Why?"...all that arrived was silence. Like all seminal moments in my life, I just had to patiently wait until the universe revealed its intentions.

A knock on the door allowed my thoughts to momentarily wander to imagine who providence might have dispatched to connect with me during and after the reading. Patience again intruded reminding me of the adage: "All good things come to those who wait."

When the door swung open, Jacki, the hostess for the evening, welcomed me with a gracious smile and then escorted me into a circle of ten waiting adults eager to hear news conveyed by one or more departed loved ones. After introducing myself and my gift of channeling, I seated myself and my energy was immediately drawn to one couple in particular with the intensity of an "electromagnetic" force.

Focusing my attention upon the husband, I told him that I saw Einstein sitting on his shoulder. Meaning? He was very very smart, a compliment which I explained and he accepted without shyness. A brief back-and-forth revealed that he was Brett Stephan Bass, a retired litigating and appellate attorney with a passion for theoretical physics and human evolution called "paleoanthropology." Then, my inner vision shifted and I saw a heart between Brett and his wife, Rosalind (Roz) Charlotte Bass. Meaning? They were soul mates. And a voice whispered from an unknown place in the universe that: "It was love at first sight! A quick marriage divinely inspired."

When I revealed this revelation to Brett, he was proud to acknowledge that he had fallen in love with Roz on their first date and, once he returned home, he had spontaneously written her a poem titled *Your Smile*. He further informed me, and the group, that he had composed three poems thereafter and presented Roz with an engagement ring on their fifth date. Teasing my talents as a psychic-medium, Brett challenged me to tell him how long he and Roz were married. All I could say with assurance was: "A long time." And his reply: "Wrong! The correct answer that every husband should give was 'not long enough,'" which evoked a chuckled from the other guests. I must admit that I've never met a couple as soul-connected as Roz and Brett Bass.

I channeled Brett and Roz and introduced them to a number of departed energies, and once I shared my gift with the remaining eight attendees, Jacki invited us all to enjoy snacks and casual conversation. It was then that I realized that my spirit guide or guides had drawn me to this gathering for a purposeful reason… to meet Brett Stephan Bass! Why? Because I had **manifested** to the guiding universal force that governs events in the cosmos that I desperately needed to meet a writer to help me to compose my biography. And Brett Stephan Bass?

In chatting with Brett following the group reading, I learned something quite amazing. At age 62, ten years ago, he had unexpectedly received the gift of "auto-writing." One day he just sat down at his computer and started to craft a 200-page novel called *Eulogy* without the benefit of an outline and without experiencing a single moment of writer's block. Apparently, a whole book, title and all, miraculously entered his mind and, in no time, was reduced to print.

As his story unfolded, Brett told me that he had just self-published his eleventh novel called *The Hand (Part I)…A Young Man's Search for Eternity's Gate* and that he was working on a sequel. When I told him that I was looking for a writer to help with my biography, he agreed to lend a **hand**, (no pun intended), and, thereafter, we collaborated on *The Hand (Part II)…A Young Man Discovers What Lies Beyond Eternity's Gate*. Now, he is helping me with this book.

Brett, Roz, and I have grown to love one another since that **fateful** introduction in 2015. It's a story worth telling in detail when the opportunity presents itself.

As I mentioned earlier, it is crucial that you accept that I have been blessed with the gift of being a psychic-medium. To add strength to my claim, and to lend value to my credibility as a professed spiritual messenger and healer, I have invited Brett to tell you about himself, his spiritual awakening, and his association with me. After he has finished, I believe that my stories of channeling will become more insightful as you weigh their validity and invite them into your future thinking.

I am Brett Stephan Bass and it is a privilege to speak directly to you at Lynn's urging. Family and friends often describe me as having a depth of knowledge, a sharp wit that features annoying puns, and a professed uninterrupted adoration for my wife. To these, I plead guilty.

Just past my 62nd birthday, in March 2009, a "gift" was left quite unexpectedly upon my intellectual doorstep. And, it has brought extraordinary joy to my life and to others.

After a compelled retirement from work at age 50 in 1997, I embarked upon a journey of self-discovery, reading over 100 books on astronomy, cosmology, quantum mechanics, human evolution, biogenesis, religion, philosophy, art, history, and other challenging topics. To add to this quest for enlightenment, I circumnavigated the globe with my wife, Rosalind (Roz), and eventually visited every continent, (including Antarctica), and what now totals more than 70 countries. Why trek around the planet? To fashion indelible "mind memories" of a world filled with a richness of history, cultural traditions, topographical splendors, and laced with people who embroider their unforgettable stories onto your heart.

A strange thing happened ten years ago. One who professed to be a psychic, stopping Roz and me in a public place, offered to share a secret that he said that he intuitively knew about me. He was not looking for money but was intent on offering what he valued to be a gift. Caught off guard, I was at a loss for words. Without waiting for my reply, he said: "You have a book in you to write" and then I gave a gratuitous "thank you" and Roz and I went on our way. Did I believe him at the time? No! The only writings etched by my pen were periodic love poems to my wife. But a book? I credited myself with neither the discipline nor the imagination needed to undertake such an elaborate enterprise. And so, the prediction was set aside to float away forever on the next available breeze until....

One year later, while sitting at my computer, my fingers began to dance on the keyboard and a month later, I wrote a semi-autobiographical novel titled "Eulogy" which I self-published to share with family and friends...true to the psychic's prediction! And five years later? I wrote, and self-published, nine additional novels: "Wind Chimes" ..."Destiny's Assassin"..."The Letter"... "The Journey"... "Why?"... "The Rivalry"... "The Bench"... "Redemption"... and "Pursuit".

In all, ten totally original self-published books in six years (available on Barnes & Noble's and Amazon's website) arriving complete in my mind's eye...no outlines ever needed; no rough drafts ever needed; no rewriting paragraphs ever needed; no writer's block ever encountered...just sit at my computer and auto-write an elegant novel in just one or two months. The process was effortless as though someone was whispering into my ear or a metaphysical power seduced the movement of the letters on my keyboard. How could this be?

At the time when I met Lynn, I had just completed my eleventh novel titled "The Hand (Part I)...A Young Man's Search for Eternity's Gate." The principal character, Emerson Alexander Weiss, proved to be a reflection of myself gazing into a timeless mirror.

I had never given much thought to spirituality at this juncture in my life until I was introduced to Lynn Van Praagh-Gratton. If the truth be told, it was Roz who was more interested in psychics than I ever was. After all, I thought I knew how the universe worked having read so many books on cosmology, astronomy, and evolutionary science.

Invited to attend Lynn's reading on October 10, 2015 by Jennie, the host's sister, Roz persuaded me to go along. Was I skeptical? Let's just say that I became excited when I was told that pizza would be served following the reading.

The session had barely begun when Lynn stared directly into my eyes. "I see Einstein on your shoulder," she said to me and my heart melted. The famous theoretical physicist was an intellectual giant who I admired greatly. Incidentally, I have a framed quote of his sitting on my office desk at home. At that moment, Lynn's message resonated with me and I opened my mind to endless possibilities...which immediately followed. [Editorial Note: Lynn did not know who was coming to the reading and neither Roz nor I are on Facebook or on any other social media sites then or now.]

Lynn then connected me to my stepfather, identifying him by his given name..."Ruben." How astounding to retrieve an unusual name completely out of thin air! She said: "He's groveling. Begging for forgiveness." And I instantly knew what his words meant since we hadn't spoken in years before his death. Then Lynn said that another man was coming forward and her description of him squarely hit the mark. It was my biological father, Benjamin, who said that he was "proud of me," and then he referenced the fact that I had become a successful lawyer.

Lynn then paused for a moment and conveyed a strange message... that the two men were arguing. It seems that my stepfather claimed that he was "the real father," which truly touched an acknowledging nerve in my mental memory. Finally, my maternal grandmother, Sophie, came through begging that I forgive her daughter, my mother, Joyce, who was still living at the time and who I hadn't spoken to in 18 years. Sophie's message was: "Please forgive your mother. You're a bigger person than she is." More came from Lynn's mouth which left me speechless. [For those who know me, the word "speechless" could never be applied to me during this lifetime.]

Thereafter, my astonishment grew exponentially when Lynn turned to Roz and delivered specific messages from her deceased brother, Jay, mother, Helen, her father, Morris, and even my grandmother, Sophie, who, in Lynn's words, said that she [Sophie] "apologized for the way my daughter, [Joyce], treated you."

A skeptic "at first," I became a believer "at last." And now knowing Lynn as I do for three-plus years, I would be first in line to vouchsafe her authenticity. Although I was given the gift of "auto-writing," she has been given an even more precious endowment…that of a psychic-medium ordained to administer healing love and to dispense reassurance that death is merely a transitional state, a way station while on an eternal journey!

What a remarkable account by Brett! One could ask: "How can complete novels suddenly appear in a person's mind to be reduced to paper, a person who claimed to lack the imagination and discipline to write a single tale of fiction?" And my reply: "How can a scant few be gifted with the ability to communicate with those who have passed and to recover messages to be shared with the living?" A plausible answer cannot be found that satisfies a curiosity and yearning to know except to quote from Shakespeare's *Hamlet*: "There are more things in heaven and earth, Horatio, than are dreamt in your philosophy." In other words, there is a deeper level of spirituality that lies in wait to greet those who pass through **Eternity's Gate**!

What distinguishes this chapter…"Stories Recovered From This Side Of Life"…from the chapter which follows…"Messages From The Other Side"? **"Physical manifestations,"** or **"signs,"** on this plane of existence which connect us to a departed energy! It could be a discovered dime…or objects moving unnaturally on a table over time…a butterfly or a cardinal arriving out of nowhere… a license plate number that begs for your attentive eye…and other signs too numerous to detail. Following this theme, let me briefly return to my encounter with Brett and Roz Bass and the aftermath before sharing stories of *"physical manifestations"* with you.

After the reading at Jacki's house concluded and goodbyes were exchanged, Brett suggested that we meet socially to get to know one another better and to discuss my need for an author to help write my biography. Weeks later, when our respective calendars permitted, Brett, Roz, and I dined together.

At dinner, Brett explained that he was writing a sequel to his novel *The Hand (Part I)…A Young Man's Search For Eternity's Gate* which was titled *The Hand (Part II)…A Young Man Discovers What Lies Beyond Eternity's Gate* and that the central figure in the continuing drama was a psychic-medium who would explain what the lead character, Emerson Alexander Weiss, discovered once he passed over to the other side. He wanted to use my biographical background and my explanation of the life-death cycle in his new book. While I wanted Brett to help me to compose a book exclusively devoted to my spiritual gift, I agreed to allow him to feature me in his Part II novel with the understanding that my life story… this book…could be written later on. And thus, *The Hand (Part II)* was written under a joint authorship. Kindly, Brett listed me ahead of himself on the cover.

Following that dinner, and as I got behind the wheel of my car, I closed my eyes and asked for a *"sign"* that I was proceeding wisely in choosing to collaborate with Brett. And, when I turned on the ignition the *"sign"* instantly was communicated through my radio speakers. It was the Beatle's 1966 song written by Paul McCartney and John Lennon called "Paperback Writer." This was a *"physical manifestation"* that my decision was prudent to receive Brett, a paperback writer, (and his wife, Roz,) into my life. Was it a mere *coincidence* that the song just happened to align itself with my desires at the moment; a song recorded by my late husband's favorite singing group? From experience, I can tell you that at critical moments during your life's journey, there are no *coincidences*! The message I received from the other side was from Dennis who was telling me: "Proceed full steam ahead!"

Since that fateful day, I have not had one single regret. I asked the universe for help and help was delivered with an added bonus attached…a friendship with Brett and Roz that has blossomed into familial caring and love!

A second "*physical manifestation*" relating to *The Hand (Part II)* is worthy of sharing because it challenges believability though it is entirely true.

The main protagonist in *The Hand* series, as noted earlier, is Emerson Alexander Weiss. One interesting thing about Emerson was that he was born with a piece of his left pinky finger missing—an explanation which is eventually revealed to the reader and married to a past life event. Nonetheless, let me continue on.

I was invited to conduct a spiritual group reading for twelve attendees in a small town in Upstate New York. It was the winter of 2017, about the time when *The Hand (Part II)* had been published. During a short break, the hostess was eager to introduce her son to me. Asking his name, he meekly replied "Emerson," which I immediately connected to the newly released novel. Jokingly, I asked those milling around whether anyone had lost part of a pinky finger. And? Sure enough, a man showed me his hand and part of a pinky was missing. **COINCIDENCE**? Emerson? Missing pinky finger?

It is easy for me to gloss over the word "*coincidence*" because I'm eager to share with you a compendium of scattered readings that highlight "*physical manifestations*" or "*signs,*" but a momentary interruption presses upon my conscience for a story deserves telling that convinces me that… The universe, or the *Source*, operates in an incomprehensibly mysterious way and that the meaning of the word "*coincidence*" conceals a greater and more profound truth shielded from the vision of man.

A HEALING MESSAGE OF
LOVE AND FORGIVENESS

[**Note**: To preserve privacy, with the single exception of my son, I will be using a first name letter when referencing the persons mentioned in this account.]

My son, Dennis Jr., as I mentioned earlier in the book, is a "sound healer," using his musical talents to bring therapeutic comfort to others. He has inherited a level of spirituality that is quite unique. Dennis lives with me and a sound studio was created in our home for Dennis to perfect his skills.

Years before the events which unfolded in this story, Dennis had a co-worker named "S" and they eventually parted ways and lost touch for more than 10 years until....

"S" recently discovered Dennis on Facebook, attracted to the fact that he had a musical gift. It seems that "S" had lost his sister, "J," in a car accident a number of years before and wanted to pay tribute to her by composing a song. Thus, Dennis seemed to re-enter his life at an important moment...by "coincidence"?... to assist in creating a heart-felt remembrance.

Know that "S's" sister, "J", had been a passenger in a car driven by a person who was under the influence of alcohol. A car crash resulted in "J's" untimely death and the driver of the car was criminally prosecuted, convicted, and sentenced to 12 years in jail.

Getting back to the tribute song, Dennis agreed to help "S" compose the song. During the creative process, both realized that the final composition was meant to be a duet and would require a male and a female vocalist. Timely..."coincidence"?... Dennis happened to know of a woman, "R," with a gifted voice, who would be perfect for the project. "S" told Dennis that he did not know "R" when her name came up in conversation.

The day that "R" was invited to the house, "S" asked me to do a reading for him. At the time, I was not aware that "R" was coming to the house and had never heard her name mentioned before. During the reading for "S," quite amazingly, "R's" name entered my mind and when it crossed over my lips, "S" was shocked... no astounded...knowing that she would be coming to the house for the first time to be auditioned for the singing part.

Here's where "coincidence" turns the corner to collide with believability! Ready?

While working on the lyrics of the song, Dennis, "S," and "R" suddenly realized that "R" was the sister of the driver of the car who had killed "S's" sister, "J!"

"COINCIDENCE?" My psychic-medium endowment informs me that the answer is a resounding "No!" From Beyond the Beyond, "S's" departed sister's energy orchestrated, (pun intended), the events to bring everyone together to deliver a healing message of "love" and especially "forgiveness" to help to erase the scar of searing pain borne by an awful tragedy.

Residing in the deepest recesses of my mind and heart is the knowledge that there is more to the word "coincidence" than we are privileged to know.

As promised, here are selected stories drawn from my vast reservoir of narratives which illustrate *"physical manifestations"* or *"signs."*

PHYSICAL MANIFESTATIONS OR SIGNS

THE LICENCE PLATE #1

[**_Note_**: I always have my cell phone camera available to document a license plate that transports, (pun intended), a message or confirmation from a place I call "**_Beyond the Beyond._**"]

My daughter, Gail, bought a pre-owned car in 2000. Purchasing a used vehicle can often mean inheriting someone else's neglectful behavior. So, was the car a "lemon" or a "peach?" Sour or sweet? Time would surrender a favorable answer in no time aided by a message sent from her father from "Beyond the Beyond!"

After properly registering the vehicle, and not interested in securing vanity plates, Gail allowed what she thought was "the luck of the draw" to determine the car's identity. And the random plate that was handed to her?

CME 6007

Meaning? "See me (CME) dad." Dennis' date of death had been June 7....6/7!

THE LICENCE PLATE #2

In early 2017, while I was driving, a friend living in Denver, Colorado, sent me a phone-link that had recorded a song that he had just written. It was dedicated to his mother and was titled…"My Angel."

When I stopped at a light, I turned on the song and was captivated by the intensity of love expressed by an adoring son for his departed mother. And then it happened as though it had been willed by the universe or, rather, the "SOURCE." A car pulled in front of me as I continued driving and its rear license plate read… "Angel"… and I immediately snapped an identifying photo to capture the fateful moment.

This was a validation from my friend's mother that she acknowledged, welcomed, and appreciated the song and its heart-expressed sentiment. Upon telling my friend about the license plate and its confirming message, he told me that it brought tears to his eyes. "Coincidence?" The odds say "no" as well as my spiritual understanding of divine purpose!

[**NOTE**: To maintain the driver's privacy, the state of issue has been removed.]

THE LICENCE PLATE #3

It was June 2019 and a friend and I were excited to attend a paid event in a restaurant where a psychic-medium would be present to do random readings. There were no assurances given that everyone would be blessed by words conveyed from the other side of death.

Well, I was privileged to be the recipient of unexpected news for the psychic-medium ventured over to my chair and told me…"You mother is here. And, she wants me to tell you that 'she's <u>here for you</u>.'" [<u>Note</u>: My mother's first name was "Regina."] And…

Two weeks later, on my birthday, June 29th, I was driving home from a reading I had just given. And… a car pulled right in front of mine and displayed a license plate which read: "<u>Regina4U</u>."

A coincidence? No! A happy birthday present sent from Beyond the Beyond.

[Photo Lost.]

THE LICENCE PLATE #4

On November 6, 1980, my brother-in-law, Gary, was in a motorcycle accident. Between November 6th and November 16th, he lay in a coma until death carried him to "Eternity's Gate."

During that stretch of ten days, I prayed for Gary's recovery knowing that hope was fading and that I would be without him for the balance of my earthly life.

While driving to his daughter's house, my mind sadly spoke to Gary and it said: "Miss you!" And... At that moment a car pulled in front of mine and its license plate read: "MisUGary."

A "coincidence?" By now, I need not supply an answer. Why? Because you already know the answer!

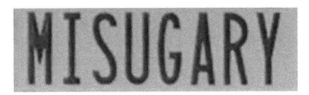

[**NOTE:** To maintain the driver's privacy, the state of issue has been removed.]

FAMILY CAR STORY

My son, Gregg, in 2017, had a passion for classic cars. Owning one was like scratching off the winning numbers on a lottery ticket. What to buy? Where to buy it? They were pressing on Gregg's psyche until his dream car caught his eye.

It was a 1972 Chevrolet Chevelle that captured his heart and threatened to empty his wallet. Was this the car to buy? A test drive would help provide the answer and Gregg wondered what his dad might have counseled. Well, the answer came once he turned on the ignition.

There was a CD in the car left by the prior owner. And the song that came on was the Beatles' "Rocky Raccoon" from their "White Album." As you may recall, Dennis was a mega Beatles fan.

The "physical manifestation" placed in a CD player was Dennis' approval stamp given to acknowledge the wisdom of his son's desires and Gregg bought the car.

RESEARCHING OUR FAMILY HERITAGE

In 2008, family members and I decided to connect to my deceased father's, Allan's, heritage that dated back more than one century to Wales. As you probably know, Wales is a country that is part of the United Kingdom and the island of Great Britain. To the east of Wales is England; to the north and west, the Irish Sea; and to the south, the Bristol Channel. It is a splendorous country boasting a coastline that stretches over 1,680 miles and is largely mountainous.

Prior to leaving, Dennis, from the other side of life, sent me an approving message that he would be with us on the trip and that "signs" would be waiting to receive us after landing on the European continent.

Once we disembarked and had retrieved our luggage, I turned to my children and said: "I wonder if my dad will send us a sign." And...? Just as I uttered these words, one of the kids pointed a finger above our heads. It read: "Go to Allan" with an arrow pointing in the direction we were walking. "Allan," my father! "Allan," a destination! A "coincidence?" I think not. A "sign?" I know so!

Anyway, we got into a taxi and soon found ourselves on a narrow dirt road. Approaching our vehicle from the opposite direction was a wide-body vehicle. To allow the vehicle to pass, *our taxi driver pulled to the side of the road. And the name on the front window of the transport vehicle? Only one word..."Dennis," written in bold block letters. And my gut told me that Dennis' energy had followed us to Wales to make our family's journey complete.*

THE BUTTERFLY

A *"physical manifestation"* can also be cathartic, washing away searing *"pain"* and *"grief"* and substituting *"acceptance"* and *"comfort."*

In 2010, I was in Denver, Colorado, for group and individual readings. It is a place that I often return to since interest in *"spirituality"* is vibrant; perhaps inspired by the Rocky Mountains to the west and the High Plains to the east.

Nevertheless, a private reading was booked with a client named Cindy W. [I will not give last names to maintain privacy]. Welcomed into a beautiful ranch-styled home, I was led to a living room couch to begin the reading and Cindy's mother instantly came through.

The message conveyed from the other side was that Cindy's mother had suffered a painful end to her life. When I revealed this fact, Cindy confirmed that cancer was the heartless culprit.

Then, in my mind's eye, I saw a butterfly. Sharing this news with Cindy, she said that both she and her mother identified with the beautiful and graceful gift created by Nature's delicate hand. And then...?

Through a window opened for ventilation,

a Monarch butterfly flew past us and headed for a hallway. And where did it land? Next to a picture of Cindy's mother that hung on a wall.

And what message did I receive to interpret the presence of the butterfly? What message needed to be shared with Cindy? I told her:

"Your mother is telling you that she is not suffering anymore. She is as free as a butterfly!"

And consolation came to Cindy. The weight of despair that had burdened her heart had been lifted and a calming peace settled in her heart then and for the days that followed.

THE CARDINAL

During the 9/11 attack on the World Trade Center, two members of the Hauppauge, Long Island, New York, Fire Department perished. Thereafter, to honor the two men, the Hauppauge Fire Department 9/11 Memorial was built at the rear of the main firehouse property.

This memorial, dedicated on September 11, 2013, was unique because it commemorated all three attack sites and incorporated into the design...a steel beam from the Twin Towers; a piece extracted from the damaged Pentagon; and shale from the crash site of Flight 93 in Shanksville, PA.

In 2015, I stopped in my car at a traffic light at the Hauppauge Fire Department 9/11 Memorial. In that moment, I shifted my eyes and saw a <u>cardinal</u> land on a glass panel which honored those lost on that horrific day. When the light turned green, I proceeded on to a group reading giving the appearance of the <u>cardinal</u> little further thought. Until?

During the spiritual group gathering, I saw in my mind's eye a mother's son and then, connecting back to the cardinal I had seen earlier, I said to one of the women: "I see a son and a cardinal around you. Does that make any sense?"

"My son was a police officer," said the mother. And I said to myself: "9/11 Memorial honoring those in service to the community like a police officer." And the relevance of the cardinal, if any?

Yes, indeed! The mother explained that when her son passed he had been living on... you may have guessed it... "<u>Cardinal</u> Lane!"

THE POCKET WATCH

At the end of 2017, I had a spiritual group reading for 12 people. I asked if anyone was a skeptic and a woman shyly raised her hand trying not to offend me. "OK," I said. "Let's see if I get a message from the other side for you."

Focusing upon the woman, I quickly received the following message:

> "I have a grandfather named 'George' here. He's showing me a pocket watch with the initial 'GCM.' On the back of the watch case is filigree on each of the four corners."

Then I hesitated to speak further because what came next made no sense at all, but I shared it nevertheless.

He's saying:

> "Why is the watch in a boot and not in a pocket?"

And the skeptical woman gasped as she proceeded to pull "George's" pocket watch from her boot...buried in her boot to hide it from my sight hoping to connect with her departed grandfather and to provide me with no advance clues.

Well, all that the stunned woman could mouth was: "Once a skeptic. Now a believer!"

THE WEEPING WILLOW TREE

During 2015, I conducted a channeling reading for a woman living in Bayside, Queens, New York. She lived in an apartment building and a rather speedy elevator delivered me to an upper floor.

Once the reading began, I immediately picked up the energy of her deceased husband. And I said quite specifically: "I see his energy surrounding a weeping willow tree."

Well, I thought the lady would keel over in shock. When I questioned her about my vision, she replied: "Look out of the window," which I did. "See," the widow began. "My son and I planted a small weeping willow tree with the permission of the apartment management to honor my late husband." And I said: "He knows and his energy will join you and your son each time you visit the planted tree."

How fitting! A "weeping" widow and son and a "weeping" tree first joined together to symbolize loss and now transformed to bring healing and comforting peace knowing that a husband-father's energy was near.

THE NEW YANKEE STADIUM

In 2009, the new Yankee Stadium replaced the original Yankee Stadium at a cost of 2.3 billion dollars and was built one block north.

It took some time for me to think about paying a visit, but the day arrived when friends invited me to join them in 2013 to attend a game. Since my Dennis was an avid Yankee fan, I decided to go to see if he would deliver a message that his energy was present, and I asked him to "send me a 'sign' that he approved of the new home of the 'Bronx Bombers.'"

During the game, a feather floated down from the cloudless sky and landed on my leg. A "heavenly" feather? Later in the game, a person four seats away yelled to someone seated 3 rows down from him. The name he yelled? Of course, "Dennis!"

Returning to my car once the game ended, I opened my driver's door, and lying on the edge of the driver's seat was? A dime—a "divine dime" to let me know that Dennis' energy had, in fact, accompanied me to the new Yankee Stadium.

How can I explain these three disparate signs? Only in one way...Dennis was with me that day and was somehow able to make his presence known!

PADRE PIO

Born on May 25, 1887, Padre Pio, also known as Saint Pio of Pietrelcina, was a friar, priest, stigmatist, and mystic. In 1999, thirty-one years after his death, he was beatified by Pope John Paul II and, three years later, canonized by the pope. The Sanctuary of Saint Pio of Pietrelcina is situated in San Giovanni Rotondo, Province of Foggia, Italy.

In 2017, my dear friend Barbara, who lives in Vermont, asked me to accompany her to her hometown in Italy where her uncle and Padre Pio did healing together. Originally eager to go, I had to cancel due to personal reasons.

Shortly thereafter, I agreed to do a reading in Pearl River, New York. And when I entered the host's kitchen, what did I see? A picture of Padre Pio. The woman explained that it hung there because her daughter prayed with devotion to the canonized saint.

Not much time passed and a friend asked me to visit a cousin's house because another medium would be present. "OK," I said. And when I was escorted into the house? On the dining room table was a statue of none other than Padre Pio. It seems that the medium was a "hands-on healer" who heals through Padre Pio.

My conclusion drawn from these two separate

events? "I couldn't visit Padre Pio, so…he came
to visit me!"

∽୧୧∽

These stories may seem farfetched; however, "*physical mani-festations*" and "*signs*" are all around us to let us know that the energy of a loved one is with us. If we allow ourselves to be "*open*" to their presence, our **conscious awareness** will be drawn to their messages. How do obscure messages seem to appear out of thin air? It is beyond my understanding to know, except to report from experience that such things are part of everyday life to be observed by those whose senses are aligned with the *frequencies of the universe* emanating from the **SOURCE**.

Concluding, there is more to "reality" than we are privy to know. It is through the good work of psychic-mediums that this veil of mystery can be lifted somewhat to try to make some sense of what lies beyond this thing we call "life on earth." So, what lies beyond this thing we call "life on earth?" My answer: "An eternal tomorrow where all *love, knowledge*, and *wisdom* reside in the illuminating *energy-light* radiating from the **SOURCE**! And thus, I end this chapter with one final story that defies logic, perhaps intended to deliver a more profound message.

THE SOURCE

As mentioned earlier in the book, I have a very dear friend named Ed. While visiting his home in 2015 something inside of me took over my brain for a moment and I involuntarily blurted out to Ed: "Get a dictionary."

Bewildered, but compliant, knowing that I often had psychic revelations, Ed retrieved a giant dictionary that most owners would have set on a pedestal for display in a room boasting a private library.

Then my mouth moved with words uttered from what must have been a celestial realm for I said, not knowing the reason or the outcome: "Without looking, I'm going to randomly point to a dictionary word that has profound meaning in my life's work."

I then proceeded to cover my eyes and asked Ed to thumb through the pages until I told him to stop, which he did while resting the heavy book on his lap. Why I said stop, I don't know. Why my pointer finger on my right hand found a particular word, I don't, for the life of me, know. All that I do know is that it happened. And the word that my finger found with shielded eyes was? "SOURCE!"

What does the word "source" mean? A definition that is usually given says: "That from which something comes into existence, develops, or derives." And, an analogy often offered is: "The Sun is our source of energy."

Well, experience gathered over a lifetime has tutored that the "SOURCE" is the source of our existence. And, through the energy of the "SOURCE," "physical manifestations" are sign-posts sent to remind us that we are on a time-less journey designed to perfect our energy so that we can eventually become "one" with the "SOURCE!"

SIX
Messages Delivered From The Other Side.

"All major religious traditions carry basically the same message, that is love, compassion and forgiveness. The important thing is they should be part of our daily lives."

Dalai Lama

Messages from the other side of life have arrived in my mind in ways that are varied and inspirational. A ***dream*** that trespasses into the future…a waking ***premonition*** of things to come… ***visual images*** waiting to be gift wrapped and then delivered to a stranger in need…and then ***whole sentences*** that demand to be written down word-for-word without undue delay to be preserved for later interpretation and contemplation.

To start, let me recover from my cell phone five messages that seemed to be dictated to me [from the ***SOURCE***?] and which I entered into my phone verbatim for future reference. Know that when each came, I felt as though I had been captured by some embracing vortex. I had no control over the thought pattern or words used. In fact, my use of language is rather straightforward and deprived of embellishment. So, when I reread the messages, I instinctively knew that I was not the author. They were crafted by one wiser and more powerful than I deserve to receive credit for! Why were they delivered? To provide inspiration and to endow me with fortitude as I continue to do healing work!

Once done, I will move on to other inspirational messages and events that are worthy of your time and reflection.

DICTATED MESSAGES FROM "BEYOND THE BEYOND"

CHANNELED MESSAGE #1
August 4, 2013
Copper Mountain, Colorado

"We are the rain waters that surround you. The time is now. We are with you and will guide you through this new endeavor. You are the rain. We are the rain. We are one and will lift you as far as the stars shine and beyond. We are one in all.

"You are ready to receive. We all are ready to bring you love from above. Safe journey. You will overcome all obstacles which will be few and far between. We love you. Follow our love. It will be a job well done preparing. Don't question. Act! Our love brought you this. Bless you. Never question who you are and why. It's not to ask. Just act and know we are here."

CHANNELED MESSAGE #2

November 20, 2013
Long Island, New York

"We are here for a short time to learn our lessons in this school called 'The Earth Vibration.' Live in love and gratitude. Be happy for what we have for we are one and blessed."

CHANNELED MESSAGE #3

June 22, 2016
Long Island, New York

"...Go forth and teach love as it will flourish in you. Well-deserved my friend."

CHANNELED MESSAGE #4

Summer 2016
Long Island, New York

"Trails of life are swept off behind you. Take heed of what is to come. It's of glory and magnificence. Behold the future of life as it will bathe you in sunshine, glory, and grace. Honor it. Respect it. And be grateful for it.

"You are a very deserving soul. Go forth and teach love as it will flourish in you. You mentor many. Only few will understand the journey. They will come to seek you out.

"Love to the fullest because there is no other way!"

CHANNELED MESSAGE #5

April 14, 2017
"Good Friday"
Long Island, New York

"Let it be known that acts of hurt and pain towards one another will not be done. Treat each other with love and honor. Walk and teach love. Do unto others. Powerful words are said but are meaningless if not used with love and from the heart from your highest being and inner soul."

I was at home when I recorded this message, sitting in my living room with a pen and paper lying close to me on a table nearby. I was watching television in the early morning hours when my ears began to ring. Instinctively, I picked up the pad and pen close at hand, calmed my emotions, and then jotted down the above words verbatim. Thereafter, I reminded myself that this was Good Friday…the Christian holiday acknowledging the crucifixion of Jesus and his death at Calvary. How fitting that I received this message on this very holy day.

Precognition has its Latin roots in *prae-*, meaning "before," and *cognitio*, meaning "acquiring knowledge." How can I, and other gifted psychics, have advanced insights into future events? It runs counter to the scientific notion that an effect cannot occur before its cause. Yet, **extrasensory perception** does exist and I stand witness as one who has experienced the phenomena on more than one occasion. Consider:

PRECOGNITION

PRECOGNITION #1
THE 9/11 ATTACK

PART I:

It was a hot summer's August day in 2001 when I embarked upon a long-anticipated and welcomed vacation that brought me to Istanbul, Turkey, and then to a dock to board a cruise ship bound for several Greek islands.

During the ride to my hotel in Turkey's capital city following my arrival, my eyes caught sight of a building, probably a mosque, which had adjacent tall towers... each with an onion-shaped crown. I learned that these were called "minarets."

Oddly, I felt instinctively that these tall towers or spires were about to be launched as rockets heading to the United States to do destructive damage. And, I feared for my homeland with a despairing concern that coursed through my body. And, in less than one month's time, the "precognitive" or "prescient" imagery would find meaning.

PART II:

On September 10, 2001, the day preceding the attack on the Twin Towers in New York City, I was working for American Airlines as a Flight

Service Manager. On that day, my friend and co-worker, Angela, and I were flying to Dallas, Texas, for a corporate meeting.

Seated on the plane's right side occupying a window seat, a sudden body chill startled my senses as I spied the Statue of Liberty below. And, I said to Angela, with words that haunt me to this very day: "I hate to see anybody do anything to the Statue."

Well, the symbol of New York City's extended arms to arriving immigrants was assaulted the following day when the two World Trade Center buildings were struck and 2,606 people died.

Why would I fear for Miss Liberty? Because the city she guarded faced imminent danger!

"Precognition" had arisen from my subconscious awareness and awakened my conscious anticipation!

PRECOGNITION #2
THE ELDERLY GREEK LADY

Following up on Part I in the previous story, leaving Istanbul, I continued my trip by taking a Mediterranean cruise which featured a guest lecturer...Dr. Brian Weiss...who I referenced in an earlier chapter. He was talking about "precognition" when suddenly an image formed in my mind. It was a short elderly Greek woman wearing a plaid dress...a mauve sweater... and flesh-colored stockings that were folded at her knees. "How strange," I remember saying to myself at the time until....

When the ship pulled into a Greek port to welcome sightseeing, what, or rather who, did I immediately see as I descended down the gangplank? You probably guessed it ...a short elderly Greek woman wearing a plaid dress... a mauve sweater...and flesh-colored stockings that were folded at her knees.

Extrasensory perception? Fact or fiction? Perhaps the story which follows will shed additional light on the subject and allow an answer to surface in your mind.

PRECOGNITION #3
HOSPITAL SCARE

One of my sons was hospitalized at age 5 because of type 1 diabetes. Stabilizing his blood sugar became a priority at that moment in time.

Having to leave the hospital as day advanced to night, my husband, Dennis, was left to comfort our son during the overnight hours. Why these parting words came to my lips, I didn't know at the time. But, I said with alarm stinging my voice: "I don't want this to be a Claus von Bülow case."

[Note: Claus von Bülow was a Danish-British socialite who was convicted of the attempted murder of his wife Sunny in 1979. An insulin overdose left her in a persistent vegetative state for the balance of her life.]

"Insulin overdose" was the haunting "premonition" which visited my mind before parting for the evening. And that night? The nurse on duty overdosed our son with insulin which sent our five-year-old into the ICU once he fell into a diabetic coma. Fortunately, he experienced a full recovery.

PRECOGNITION #4
A CHANCE MEETING?

In March 2019, I was on my way to meet a friend for lunch in Queens, New York, about 30 miles from my home. Looking at my fuel tank gauge, I realized that I needed a fill-up before venturing so far.

As I made my way to the gas station, my mind visualized meeting someone I hadn't seen in three years. And then, I silently listened and an inner voice said: "Funny if I see him in the gas station pumping gas." And an image of him doing just that was painted by my brain.

Well, you guessed it! As I pulled into the station my head turned right. And? There he was filling his tank as I had foreseen minutes earlier. We exchanged pleasantries after I blurted out: "This is weird!" And he, equally surprised to see me, responded: "God!"

Upon leaving, I whispered two words to myself: "premonition" and "SOURCE."

EXTRASENSORY PERCEPTION

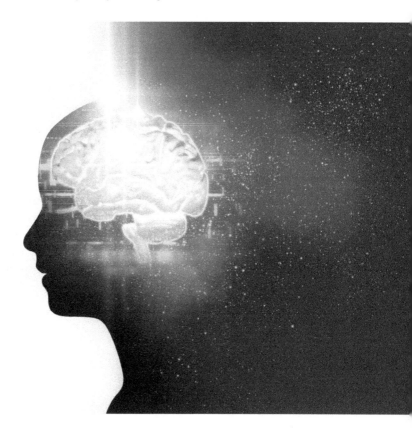

SUICIDE REVEALED
September 10, 2001
Dallas, Texas

The night that Angela and I arrived in Dallas for the American Airlines business conference, I felt uneasy and admittedly frightened. The hotel where we were staying was an old turn-of-the-century building which perhaps led to the creepy feelings that caused my heart to skip more than one rhythmic beat.

I was picking up the presence of "negative" energy and I was scared. So, I imposed upon my friend's privacy and asked Angela if I could spend the night in her room. Was I picking up the 9/11 attack-to-be or something else?

The next afternoon, a rooftop luncheon was arranged for the conference's attendees. When I reached the rooftop, my mind suddenly shared a long-forgotten secret that the hotel's management was happy to conceal from its guests. Namely, my conscious understanding informed me that someone, likely a woman in her 50's, either died on the roof or jumped to her death.

Later that day, I went to the concierge desk and asked about the message that crept into my waking thoughts. And a kind gentleman said: "At the turn of the 20th century, a woman did commit suicide by leaping from the roof."

Sharing with him the fact that I was a psychic-medium, he shared with me another secret not openly publicized. He told me that there was a room in the hotel where séances had been held. "Do you want to see the room," he asked with excitement. And I said: "Yes!"

Leading me down a corridor heading to the room, a spirit's energy stopped me in my tracks and I realized that to enter the room would be to risk being besieged by "negative" energy... like playing with a Ouija board. So, I proceeded no further, warning my chaperone that visiting the room was not a good idea.

My message to you? Take heed of the adage:

"To be forewarned is to be forearmed!"

Let me conclude this chapter with just a sprinkling of additional messages delivered to me from **Beyond the Beyond** intended to implant **hope**, **love**, and **acceptance** in the grieving hearts of others.

ADDITIONAL MESSAGES RETRIEVED FROM "BEYOND THE BEYOND"

THE HEATHER BUSH

When I retired from my position at American Airlines, I became an assistant to the Treasurer of the Stagehands' Union in Manhattan. In 2016, there was a day when background music was playing in the office and my ears picked up Louis Armstrong's classic rendition of "What a Wonderful World" on the radio. And, my attention suddenly shifted to a woman named "Winnie" and a picture formed in my mind.

I saw Winnie running through a field of heather on a bright sunny day. There was a small boy and girl holding each of Winnie's hands. And Winnie had the most ebullient smile on her face.

I have a close client-friend, Carol, who lives in Colorado and, at the time, her mother Winnie was 93. Winnie was quite a character. Suffice it to say that she continued to ski until she was 89.

Why did "What a Wonderful World" trigger thoughts of dear sweet Winnie? Well, the answer came that day when my cell phone rang. It was Carol to deliver sad news. Winnie had passed away.

When I gained my composure, I silently sent a message to Winnie wherein I said: "Send me a 'sign' from the other side." And?

The next day a florist rang my doorbell at home. He was delivering a "heather bush." Heather like my vision of Winnie frolicking in a field on the other side of life!

Looking for a note. I found none! Why? Because intuitively I knew that Winnie was the sender letting me know that she was all right so that I could forward the message along to her daughter, which I did!

How can I explain this bizarre experience? In all honesty, I can't, in good conscience, offer a "logical" or "rational" explanation in human perception terms. The answer, therefore, must reside elsewhere...no doubt a place which I've come to call "Beyond the Beyond!"

A BOY'S WISH

It was 2015 and I was doing a spiritual group reading in a restaurant called "Pompeii" in West Hempstead, New York. There were many eager faces waiting for a message from one or more people who had passed.

Opening up a receptive mind to welcome energies to join the group, a young boy of five came through to me wearing a fireman's helmet which was black in color. [Note: I do see colors when I channel.] The young child was seated in a toy fire truck and his face glowed with delightful joy.

When I asked if this resonated with anyone, a mother acknowledged that it was her son who had left this earth too soon in life. She shared with us his fervent desire to become a fireman and informed us that he had been honored by the Elmont, New York, Fire Department which graciously named him "Fireman for a Day" and let him take a seat on a hook and ladder truck to allow his tender mind to fantasize about being a real fireman.

Like Winnie in the previous story, this young boy too found peace and tranquility in a place I call "Beyond the Beyond." Each let me know that he/she was all right through "visual images" that, when conveyed, would strike a receptive cord in the hearts of those left behind.

ANOTHER BOY RELIVING HIS DREAM

It was a 2014 spiritual group reading in yet another restaurant, a typical venue for me. There were 12 women seated at the table. Again, typical. Where are the husbands hiding? Anyway, excuse the digression.

I connected to several people who had entered "Eternity's Gate," but one stuck in my mind for weeks after the reading. He was an eight-year-old boy.

[Note: I do so many readings and have channeled so many stories, it's truly hard to remember one from another. Much like you might strain to remember what you had for dinner three nights ago since so many meals collide.]

The young boy was dressed head-to-toe in a baseball uniform and he was standing in the center of a large baseball stadium. He was saying that he was playing with the best...Casey Stengel, Lou Gehrig, Mickey Mantle. [Note: Clearly a Yankee fan in life.]

"Does this register with anyone?" I asked. And a mother with tears starting to flow down her cheeks said: "Yes! My son was buried in his baseball uniform."

Yet another <u>symbolic</u> "visual image" for someone to find comfort in receiving, knowing that a loved one's energy had endured and was eternal.

THE TWO TEACHERS

On February 14, 2018, Nikolas Cruz opened fire at Marjory Stoneman Douglas High School in Parkland, Florida. Wielding an AR-15 style rifle, he killed 17 students and staff members and wounded 17 others. Two or three days thereafter, I had a group spiritual reading in Woodside, Queens, New York, for 10 people. Yes... again all women!

Strangely, I felt the energy of the slain Parkland children once I started the reading. Why?

Focusing what I call my "third psychic eye," I felt the spinning energy presence of two relatively young women. "Teachers," I silently whispered to myself. And then a message came from both, joined as one, which I shared with the group.

> "We worked with children on earth and now on the other side we're helping them. We want to connect two mothers who are strangers so that they can find peace together."

The relevance of the message? Two women had each lost a daughter who had been a teacher. One died in her 30's of cancer. The other passed in her 40's as a result of a car accident.

When the night ended, both grieving mothers hugged and exchanged contact information. The healing had finally begun in earnest for both thanks to their daughters who had bonded on the other side and who conveyed a shared message of love!

THE BOMBER JACKET

In 2015, I was invited to a hotel in Colchester, Vermont, to conduct a group reading for what turned out to be 200 attendees. Colchester is a suburb of Burlington and is located on the shore of Malletts Bay, part of Lake Champlain.

During the session, I said: "I have a man here named 'Jack' and he's telling me something about his World War II bomber jacket. Does this make sense to anyone? He's showing me the jacket and emphasizing that he wore it during the war and that there is a story that needs to be told tonight."

Two ladies, neither knowing that the other was coming to the readings, instantly connected to the frequency-energy who I identified as "Jack." And this is the story they told me and shared with the group as Jack had wanted.

One of the two ladies was shopping at a local thrift shop when she spotted a bomber jacket hung on a rack. Checking the condition, she noticed a name inside the garment. In an extraordinary act of charity, the lady bought the jacket hoping to return it to the owner's family or descendents, if possible. To do so, she put an ad in the local newspaper. And...?

It seems that the second lady present had read the ad and recognized her dad's name, realizing that it was his World War II bomber jacket. And the rest became history and an anecdote worth repeating!

The jacket was returned to a veteran's daughter; the two ladies developed a friendship for life; and Jack's story was recounted to the group as he so fervently desired that evening...delivered from a place called "Beyond the Beyond" where one day we will all call home!

HEART-TO-HEART

In 2018, on Long Island, New York, I conducted yet another group reading. And, I said: "A son is coming through. He says that he's around his mother and he has just explained the reason behind his passing." [A reason I choose not to disclose here because of the pain attached.]

"He's repeating that he's always around his mother and is acknowledging a 'round disc attached to a necklace with his photo enclosed wearing a baseball cap.' And then he's saying: 'My heart is always next to mom's heart. I will always be with her.'"

A woman, with tears forming in her eyes, then pulled a silver disc attached to a silver chain from her blouse. She said that it held a picture of her beloved son wearing a baseball cap. And...next to the disc was a silver locket shaped like a heart which she said held some of her son's ashes which explained why he said, when I channeled his words: "My heart is always next to mom's heart. I will always be with her."

THE TATTOO

During a recent Long Island spiritual reading, a father came through for a young man in his 30's attending the session. The deceased man wanted to "validate" his presence by offering a message that only his son could understand and had stored away in his aching heart.

The frequency-energy called himself "Pat" and then he/it said something quite specific. "Ask my son to show you his tattoo on his leg. It's a crucifix with my name on it."

Shocked at first, the young man in question gained his composure and proceeded to pull his left pant leg up to reveal on his calf...a black tattoo with the name "Pat" etched across it in bold block lettering.

Other messages soon followed but "validation" was all that really mattered in the end because...it confirmed that death is not an ending. Thus, this message was intended to bring long-lasting healing solace to the sensibilities of a grieving son.

UNREQUITED LOVE...
<u>PINK ROSES</u>

It was a spiritual group gathering in Upstate New York in 2018. Several frequencies channeled their messages as the intended recipients acknowledged that the stories resonated with them. Then, I said: "<u>Jim</u> is here. He's carrying a bouquet of pink roses for someone who is about to celebrate a birthday. Again, he's showing me the pink roses in order to emphasize their symbolic importance to someone. Is anyone about to have a birthday? Do the pink roses have a more profound meaning?"

Well, a woman chimed in that her birthday was the next month, and she then proceeded to share an astonishing story with those present.

"I was single and worked as a bartender," she began. "For two years, a man secretly managed to leave a bouquet of pink roses for me on the bar counter, on a regular basis, before I arrived at work. How he kept it a secret for so long, I can't explain. But, he did!

"One day, he got the courage to formally introduce himself to me. Although I remembered his face, I didn't recall his name until he told me it was '<u>Jim</u>' and admitted that he had a crush on me and had left me the roses. I expressed my appreciation, of course, but suggested that I was dating someone else to politely dismiss the prospects of a relationship.

"Some time later, I learned that <u>Jim</u> had passed and felt somewhat guilty that I didn't have the same feeling for <u>Jim</u> as he had had for me."

I then told the lady that: "<u>Jim</u> is bringing forth love to you and you should not carry the regrets of survivor's guilt."

This story is an account of unrequited love… love given but not returned, but…in the end, love is never truly lost for it waits for you, in all its eternal beauty, in a place called "Beyond the Beyond!"

THE MASS CARD

A glorious sapphire sky, which offered a warmth that caressed my face, welcomed my arrival one afternoon in July 2019. Visiting my friend Ed's home which overlooked a serene lake that barely sported a ripple, we chatted in a screened-in porch enjoying one another's company.

Sometimes, when I'm least expecting a visitor to arrive from "Beyond the Beyond," one might simply pop in and deposit a message in my mind to pass along. And that's what happened that summer's day.

I turned to Ed and said: "I keep hearing the name Ralph Waldo Emerson. I think your mother is here."

Leaping from his seat with a mission that could not be delayed, Ed ran to his bedroom and retrieved a mass card he had chosen to honor Mae, his beloved mother, who had passed on June 6, 2006. And the quote which he showed me on the card? A poem titled "Success" penned by Ralph Waldo Emerson.

A ONE AND ONLY EXPERIENCE

As I recount this story, I pause to take a deep breath for nothing like what I'm about to share with you has ever happened to me before or after.

In 2019, in Suffolk County, Long Island, New York, I came to a woman's home who had invited me to do a reading eight years before. This time, however, bore greater purpose since the woman had just lost her husband within the past 60 days.

It seems that the wife and her husband had two dogs, one which was particularly fond of the now deceased husband and who paid very little, if any, attention to his wife.

When we began the session, the wife said something that nearly knocked me off my seat: "I think my husband is in the dog who loved him but not me." When I asked why, she replied: "He never paid attention to me before, but now he does. He hops in bed with me. He is constantly by my side." On and on and on, she described behavior that was most unusual and loving given the dog's past indifference displayed towards her.

And then the reading got into full swing and the wife's husband came through. And when I started to talk about her husband, the aforementioned dog began to make strange sounds which, for the life of me, I can't mimic on paper. It was bizarre.

Even more bizarre is when I shifted the reading away from referencing the husband, the dog grew silent. BUT...channeling the husband's words again, the dog's voice could not be quieted.

Then I told the grieving widow: "I'm going to talk about grandma." And the dog? Got up and left the area displaying an apparent annoyance. Once I concluded and resumed talking about her husband again, who showed up making strange noises? You guessed it. The dog!

Crazy as it sounds, I believe that the widow was somewhat correct when she said that her late husband was in the dog. My interpretation is that her husband's energy flowed through the dog and was picked up by my psychic-medium antennas to relay a husband's love to his wife. If you ask me for another explanation, I'm left speechless.

THE VIETNAM VET

In 2018, just recently as I sat down to begin writing this book, I was invited for a social lunch with a Vietnam Veteran named John and his lovely wife, Evelyn; both friends. Little did I know that the war survivor carried regrets in his heart that couldn't be dismissed in 49 years. It was a story that he had kept bottled-up inside, refusing to share it with me and others.

This was not intended to be a psychic reading, but sometimes messages are delivered to me for a profound healing purpose without prompting.

"I see a <u>Mack</u> truck," I blurted without taking a breath. "I see something associated with the opposite of 'high,'" I uttered, and then realized the word that I was searching for was <u>low</u>. "I see a man flipping a 'Zippo' lighter, a reusable metal lighter which became popular with the United States military."

What did it all mean? A secret stored away for decades finally surfaced.

My friend said that his buddy in the patty fields of Vietnam-Cambodia was Lomax—blending my "low" and "Mack" references. Lomax had been killed in action while my friend had survived.

John then recounted the events in vivid detail as though he was momentarily escorted back in time.

"I was dispatched to the Vietnam War, (from 1969-1970), and Lomax and I eventually found ourselves facing an enemy in a fierce combat zone in Cambodia in 1970. During a lull in the fighting, a helicopter came which took me back to our field base, leaving Lomax behind, which I was reluctant to do. In my gut, I feared I would never see him again. [<u>Author's Note</u>: Premonition?]

"When I arrived at the field base, I was told that my father had died and that I was being sent back to the 'real world,' my home in the states. The image of Lomax stayed with me and I visualized him flipping his Zippo lighter to light cigarette after cigarette.

"Once home, news arrived that my friend and comrade, Lomax, had been 'KIA'...killed in action. While I now have come to believe that my father's death had saved my life, because it is likely that I would have died alongside Lomax, I am not at peace because I carry what is called 'survivor's guilt...why him and not me?'"

Then, with John's permission, I continued to jot down his agony-laced words.

"For so many years, I have tried to live with

the guilt...to suppress those feelings that many of us will take with us forever. At age 18 years old, I should not have had to carry these feelings of guilt forever.

"Those who are survivors, who come out of harm's way alive, need to protect our emotions in order to stay alive. Lynn, knowing that Lomax is still with me all of the time, and that he watches over me, gives me great comfort. It helps me to release the anger that I hold within!

"Why him and not me?" John challenged all reason. Survivor's guilt had shadowed John and it refused to stop tormenting him for seemingly endless years.

[**Postscript:** Survivor or survivor's guilt, also referred to as survivor or survivor's syndrome, is real and is not to be blithely dismissed as simply "something that can be mentally extinguished over time." Recently, the medical community has identified it as a "significant symptom of post traumatic stress disorder (PTSD)."]

In this reading, combat memories resurfaced with a soldier surviving a traumatic event...the death of a brother-in-arms. However, survivor's guilt also extends to those who bear witness or are touched by deaths resulting from epidemics, terrorism, murder, natural disasters, and suicide just to recount a few.

We often hear this guilt-ridden refrain from Holocaust survivors or 9/11 survivors or combat veterans returning home from the current conflict in Iraq and Afghanistan: "Why him or her and not me?" This remorse burrows deep into the heart unwilling to peacefully exit.

Symptoms of the condition often include unsettling feelings, troubling thoughts, and disturbing dreams that refuse to leave the person reliving a harrowing memory. And the by-product? Both physical and mental anguishing disrupting distress!

Can I, a spiritual healer, bring calming peace to one suffering from survivor's guilt? In the reading that I conducted to connect my friend to his buddy Lomax, I did take the first step in the healing process, leaving more work to be done by those professionals skilled in treating the lingering syndrome. My message from the reading was that we are all born with a pre-written life script attached to our DNA before we arrive on this earthly plane of existence. Why did Lomax die so young? I don't deign to know. Perhaps Lomax's death was preordained to teach his friend a life lesson that would serve as a guiding hand in coloring in the tapestry of what was meant to be his life story.

In sum, we must live our lives free of survivor's guilt when we are not accountable for the events surrounding a given death or deaths. This was a teaching moment for the Vietnam survivor in part because the good news is that one day he and Lomax will be reunited in a place that I've come to call ***Beyond the Beyond.***

Time to move on hoping that you are now convinced that…
YOU MUST LIVE LIFE WITHOUT FEARING DEATH!

SEVEN
Living Life Without Fearing Death

"Live your life that the fear of death can never enter your heart."

Tecumseh

What has being a psychic-medium taught me about death? That it is an illusion!

If you lived your life with the fear of death being wiped away like a tear being absorbed by a tissue, would you live your life differently? Would you dispense with mourning for the loss of a loved one because you knew that one day you would be reunited? Would you challenge your mind to try to understand your purpose for living? Well, that's where my gift surfaces to offer reassurance and guidance that your time on earth is transitional. Meaning? You are like a rainbow.

A "rainbow?" you might question evincing confusion. Well, let me explain my strange analogy.

A rainbow is a spectrum of light appearing as a multi-colored circular arc of seven glorious colors—red, orange, yellow, green, blue, indigo, and violet. If you joined all seven colors together to allow them to become *one*, what color would emerge? *WHITE!* And so, let me return to my analogy.

The *Source* is pure illuminating *white light*—something that we each strive to become to achieve eternal *love, knowledge*, and *wisdom*. We are each a journeyman/journeywoman born with impurities in our energy intensities. How can we rid ourselves of the impurities, or what we may call "vices" or kindly "imperfections" that corrupt our character? By living...dying...and being reborn so that we can learn life lessons along the way that increases the frequency of our *eternal energy*.

Consider each color of our individual rainbow to be a reborn life experience. There is first the red experience when basic lessons are learned followed by a *reincarnated* orange rebirth...then a yellow...then a green...then a blue...then a indigo...and finally a violet when all life experiences/lessons merge together to become *one*...pure *WHITE!* When this occurs, rebirth fades from meaning and we find eternal contentment in a place I call *Beyond the Beyond* where a final journey begins—to become "*one*" with the *Source*.

Recently, I conducted a reading for one knowledgeable in physics. He had accompanied his significant other who, to be blunt, twisted his arm to join her in trying to connect to the other side. As one fascinated by science, he was skeptical, to say the least, that voices residing beyond the grave could be invited to join the living. Well, when all was said and done, having been visited by several family members residing on the other side, he scratched his head and said with a shy reticence: "You've converted a non-believer into a believer!"

I asked him how he could apply his knowledge of science to the reading I had just conducted; namely, *energy* or *consciousness* surviving to live on. And he immediately said: "The First Law of Thermodynamics." Asked to explain, he said these words which, with his permission, I recorded for future reference.

The First Law of Thermodynamics has to do with the law of conservation of energy which teaches that the total energy of an isolated system has to be constant. To simplify the concept, the first law means that energy can be transformed from one form to another, but cannot be created or destroyed.

If you rub your hands together quickly while pressing down hard you'll feel heat coming off your palms. You're not creating energy, rather, you're moving the chemical energy of your body...carrying it through your muscles and into your hands. You haven't created energy. You've just moved it around.

Then I asked him how his thinking made sense of his reading. He paused for a good length of time until a smile emerged on his face and he said in a whispering tone that caused me to lean forward as I continued to record his words:

The First Law of Thermodynamics is also intertwined with the structure of the universe—the planets, the solar system,

*the galaxy and galaxies act in concert with the principle. So…
so…(a hesitation)… if human consciousness exists, which it
clearly does, then it cannot be destroyed. It must survive!*

I'm a psychic-medium…not a scientist, especially one who
struggled mightily to get a passing grade in chemistry in high
school let alone advance to physics. However, thinking about what
my client said, I can weave his message into my life experiences of
channeling the messages of those who have passed. And my conclusion? "Death? Conservation of energy? ***Consciousness***, or the
energy housed in the human body, can't die but can be reborn in
some interconnected cycle of existence!"

So, let me return to the chapter heading: "Living Life Without
Fearing Death." What wisdom can I impart to you from my countless readings accumulated over four decades?

Live each day allowing joy to flow into your heart! How…
through continuous acts of kindness, both small and more robust!
Give bountiful love to family members and charity to strangers
so that you can receive bountiful love and charity in return which
will enhance the colors of your unique rainbow! Put petty differ-
ences aside and seek healing reconciliation! Live each moment in
the present without fear of the future! Awake each morning with
optimism! Pause some time during a hectic day and try to connect
with nature's grandeur…a star-laden sky, the voice of a sparrow
carried on a breeze, resplendent colors delivered to the eyes by a
gardener's plantings! Spend a quiet moment in each day reserved
just for tranquil meditation and a heart-inspired prayer! Look for
signs that your loved ones are around you. And, most especially,
don't fear death for the thought will diminish your celebration of
life!

EIGHT
Finding Love's Enduring Eternal Virtue

"To love someone is nothing. To be loved by someone is something. To love someone who loves you is everything."

Bill Russell

Over the course of a lifetime, I've heard the word "love" diminished in value by overuse! Consider: "I love the smell of a fresh baked apple pie as soon as it comes out of the oven. I love to sleep really late on my one day off. I love to go to a Broadway show, especially a musical-comedy. I love the color of the nail polish I'm wearing even if my husband thinks that it's hideous. I love to do the *Sunday Times* crossword puzzle every week even when it's impossibly hard to complete. I love to go two or three days without shaving even though my wife tells me I look like a bum. Sometimes, I just love to stay put and just do nothing. I love the New York Yankees and attending a game in person. I love a discounted bargain. I love to dance…to sing…to tell jokes. I love an ice cold beer when the summer sun fries me like a steak on the grill. I love it when we turn the clocks forward and daylight grows stronger and longer. I love it when the kids are finally asleep and I can at last quiet my mind and my body. I love it when my accountant tells me that I'm getting a tax refund and I spend it in my brain before it reaches my hand. I love it when my car is clean after a rainstorm…my refrigerator is full after returning from a vacation…my ironing is done after hours of standing." I *love*…I *love*…I *love*…I *love*…I *love*…. *Love* is not a word to be used casually. Why? Because it is the essence of *"cleansing purity,"* a gift of *"spiritual holiness"* emanating from the **Source**.

Love is what living is all about…here on earth and in **Beyond the Beyond**. You cannot become *"one"* with the **Source** unless you surrender totally to the eternal nourishment of *"celestial love."* It is like the air you inhale to survive as a human…the nutrients that sustain your body while your **consciousness** prepares you for a "life-death-life" cycle…it is, in two words, *"eternal ecstasy."*

Do we experience what I call *"eternal ecstasy"* on this third planet from the Sun? Momentarily, like the flames of birthday candles extinguished by a strong breath. Examples? Four come to mind.

(1) Moments after the birth of a child when he or she is placed in her mother's comforting embrace for the very first time.

(2) When those gather around a dying loved one to bring solace and closure.

(3) The first kiss shared by a couple who are predestined to become soul mates.

(4) When, in the heat of battle, with bullets flying everywhere, a soldier risks his his own life and carries a wounded comrade to safety.

Experience in conducting countless readings has taught me that somehow *light* and *love* are bound together, twins born of the same source which I've come to know as the ***Source***. To eventually become "***one***" with the ***Source*** means to immerse one's *energy* with *its* radiating perfection—bathing one in resplendent *light* that communicates transcendent *love*.

Each time that we die and are carried off to ***Beyond the Beyond***, our *energy* or *consciousness* is guided by a carriage of illuminating *light* that makes our passing one deprived of fear. Those who have had a near death experience invariably recount being guided by *light* and embraced by *love*.

Thus, the point of this chapter is: To encourage you to choose *love* over anger...to amplify your *love* by never losing the opportunity to express it, in words and in deeds, to those near and dear...to offer charity to the lives of those who are in need...by tempering your ego and your material desires in search of a deeper and more profound spirituality. And by doing? Well, you can fill in the "and by doing" as it pertains to your current life's journey and resources!

NINE
Eternity Awaits
With Open Arms.

"We are travelers on a cosmic journey, stardust, swirling and dancing in the eddies and whirlpools of infinity. Life is eternal. We have stopped for a moment to encounter each other, to meet, to love, to share. This is a precious moment. It is a little parenthesis in eternity."
— Paulo Coelho

Does the name Rodrigo de Triana suggest anything to you? Here's a hint that would have meant something to Rodrigo but likely very little to you. He was born Juan Rodrigo Bermejo in 1469 in a small town in Spain. Here's a further hint to invite your curiosity to know more. He was a sailor whose claim to historical fame was eclipsed by his captain's false entry into a journal. Does *La Pinta* bring you closer to an answer? Well then, let me explain because I'm sure that my clues seem to be nothing more than foolish teasing.

La Pinta, translated from Spanish to connote *The Painted One* or *The Look* or *The Spotted One*, began a transatlantic voyage in 1492 along with two other vessels. They were headed to "discover" the *New World*, which had long before been discovered by a number of native tribes who would challenge the word "discover."

On October 12, 1492, Rodrigo, a lookout on the *La Pinto*, captured sight of land which the inhabitants called Guanahani, an island in the Bahamas which his captain, Christopher Columbus, would later call "San Salvador." At about 2:00 A.M., Rodrigo de Triana cried out…"*¡Tierra! ¡Tierra!*" (Land! Land!). In his log, Columbus took credit for first casting an eye upon the island leaving one to decry his deceit as ego-driven!

"So," you ask, "what is the point of the story?" That those in power positions often act without a moral "compass"…pun intended. No, although there is merit in the statement.

What lay over the **horizon** when the *La Pinta* left port? No one knew until the journey began and the three separate crews sailed into uncertain waters. And what lies over the **horizon** for each of us when our body withers away and death arrives? My response—a realm called **Beyond the Beyond** which, unlike you, I have visited courtesy of countless energies who have passed through **Eternity's Gate** and shared their voices and their stories with me.

I recently came across an inspiring quote that I'm anxious to share with you. It is extracted from a poem called *Death is Only an Horizon* penned in 1910 by Rossiter Worthington Raymond

(1840-1918), an American mining engineer, legal scholar, and gifted author:

> *Life is eternal; and love is immortal; and death is only a horizon; and a horizon is nothing save the limit of our sight.*

We have grown accustomed to measure moments in sequential time. But, in truth, time is but an invention of man to manage his affairs and to catalog his memories. I have learned that in the realm called *Beyond the Beyond* time loses all meaning and is replaced by the word "*eternity.*"

The *real* you is born of "*energy,*" not flesh. What we call flesh is like the shell that houses the chick (*energy/consciousness*) that will one day hatch. We emerge into earth's life for a time to strive to work towards perfection. It may take one, two, three, or countless rebirths to achieve some semblance of "*purity of purity,*" but once we do, our *energy* (or *frequency* or *consciousness*) gains a certain modulation and our earthly journey ends and our celestial one continues on in an astral realm which, by now, you know I call *Beyond the Beyond*. Here, we are challenged to further increase/ elevate/perfect our *energy* to pair with that of the *Source's*. How long will it take? The question is meaningless because time ceases to exist on the other side and surrenders itself to the endlessness of eternity.

The lesson here is clear. Fear not death for existence is eternal. Celebrate life on earth with love and charity to abbreviate your short-term/long-term stay. Why? Because your eternal home is not here and now. It is destined to be in the welcoming reunion with the *Source*!

TEN
Prepare In Life For Forever's Tomorrows.

"Be prepared to be on the race to fulfill and to achieve fulfillment."
✑ Sunday Adelaja

Thank you for taking this journey with me and, hopefully, placing your trust in me. Throughout the breadth of my life it has been my heart which has guided my desires and my actions. I was given a psychic-medium gift, a gift not of my own choosing. The use I have made of it, however, has been, and continues to be, of my own choosing—to bring **comfort**, **hope**, and **understanding** to those who have lost a loved one or to those fearing the arrival of death in their own lives.

This chapter concludes with these instructive words drawn from a lifetime of channeling the messages of those who now reside **Beyond the Beyond**. "Prepare in life for forever's tomorrows" is a clarion call for each of us to study our reflection in an introspective mirror. Do you find contentment in the face staring back at you? If not, then why not? If so, have you underestimated your ability to be an even better person than you judge yourself to be?

To connect to the **Source**, you must perfect your **energy** by attracting and dispensing **LOVE** starting in this world and carrying it over beyond the unseen horizon. How you achieve it is up to you. There is no single recipe. My close friend and collaborator, Brett Stephan Bass, tells me that the acronym **SEA** should be employed in the pursuit of **love**. He says it stands for a "**S**pontaneous **E**xpression of **A**ffection." Meaning? Surprise one with an unexpected gift of **love** like…flowers delivered out of the clear blue, not just reserved for a special holiday or birthday…a "thinking of you" card to a dear friend who you haven't connected with for way too long…an extra large cash tip placed in a server's hand who went out of his/her way to please…a contribution to a charity sent before a request is made…a kind word to a stranger on the street who allows you to pass because you're in a mad-dash rush…by allowing one in a checkout line with few groceries to get in front of you when your basket is full…an unexpected kiss on the cheek, pat on the back, or encouraging word to show that you truly care.

I assure you, acts of goodness add up over a lifetime and will serve you well when you reach **Eternity's Gate**. It has enduring worth that may tip the scales to signal whether you will stay in a celestial place or your ***energy/consciousness*** will be dispatched back to earth to enrich what many religions call your "***soul***."

The time to act is now! Look ahead and not behind because the past is already engraved in the ***Book of Your Life's Story*** while tomorrow is still left uncharted and unwritten.

Know that you are not alone! Those who have passed are still around you. Look for ***divine dimes*** for it is their way of letting you know that their ***love*** for you has never faltered nor faded. Man's journey is clouded in mystery; but, through my words, I hope that the veil of uncertainty has been lifted somewhat to provide you with comforting reassurance that ***tomorrows are forever***!

Epilogue

In the introduction to this book titled "My Journey Is Your Journey," I wrote these words:

Before I began to consider assembling my thoughts needed to piece together my life story, I went to a local Long Island beach to ask the eternal energy of the universe, which I have come to know as the "Source," to allow me to begin a journey of remembrance and to share my life experiences with others.

Having composed what seemed like the last lines of this book, I laid it aside for a time to allow the experience to achieve a certain closure like I do after conducting a reading for one in need of reassurance. This morning, I retrieved the manuscript from a drawer and held it without opening it. What I felt was indescribable radiating *love* that coursed through me like an electric shock. Energy sent from *Beyond the Beyond?* Perhaps. And then a voice softly whispered in my conscious awareness: "Take the book to be beach. Sit upon the rock that provided your original inspiration. And, let your mind wander." And, I did just that.

It was late in the day when summer vanished and those visiting the beach were few in numbers. A cool breeze greeted me and I felt refreshed physically and spiritually. In the distance, I spotted that isolated rock and quickly advanced as though an old friend awaited my arrival. And...my heart began to race with excitement and anticipation.

Seating myself, I took a deep breath and closed my eyes and the scent of saltwater greeted my sense buds for a brief moment. Then, I felt myself lift off the rock as though I were a rocket being launched into space to explore some unknown region of our galaxy. With eyes still closed, my inner vision witnessed a burst of extraordinary *white light* which seemed to illuminate what my mind told me was the eternal universe. And, I felt the purity of *perfected love*...peace and contentment, I judged, sent from the *SOURCE*!

Had I escaped reality to be brought to a deeper reality of

understanding? I believe so because when my eyes involuntarily opened wide, I saw a hazy mist way off in the direction of the horizon. And, the message that I felt it conveyed was that my life's work as a psychic-medium had resonated with my destiny to become a "*healer of hearts*."

There is still so very much for me and for you to do for the world suffers greatly from unending inhumanity. My journey is your journey. Let us all work together to try to change things for the better…to strive to create a kinder tomorrow as we remember that the highest achievement to be attained is to become "*one*" with the *SOURCE!*

In closing, let me share one final "*profound*" story that defies rationale explanation. In its essential details, however, it tutors why I am alive and what divine purpose has colored and continues to color my advancing years.

Epilogue

AN ANGELIC VISITATION?

Two days before I was to leave to conduct spiritual healing sessions in Colorado, I went to church to light a candle to be placed with reverence beside Mother Mary's statue. This was intended to express my devotion to her and to invigorate my frequency-energy as I prepared to undertake a "healing" journey.

When my jet took off for Denver, it was Sunday, February 1, 2015...Super Bowl XLIX when the New England Patriots would play the Seattle Seahawks in Glendale, Arizona. And, I learned that the pilots were anxious to arrive in Denver on time, or even earlier, to watch the game on television. Perhaps this explains why we arrived 30 minutes before the scheduled arrival time.

When I disembarked, I gathered my belongings and eventually waited by the curb for a pre-arranged ride to take me to my hotel. Looking at my watch, I realized that I had 30 minutes to kill so I decided to wait comfortably inside the terminal.

All of the interior waiting areas were constructed of glass and a person's vision was not obstructed in any direction. You could see everything going on for great distances. Why I mention this will shortly become apparent.

Finding my way to a comfortable row of seats, I spotted a lady dressed in the most vibrant color of purple and my feet carried me over to her almost involuntarily. She remarked favorably about my blue clothing and I returned the compliment about her stunning attire.

"You are a vision of light," exclaimed the
stranger to me.
"Thank you for doing God's service!"

Needless to say, I was shocked by the woman's intuition about my life's calling.

Seating myself beside the lady, we began to talk and she volunteered that she worked with the homeless all over the country. And I replied: "I do spiritual healing."

The woman then asked what my name was and I said "Lynn." And she replied: "Your name means 'light.'" Inquiring about her name, she said: "Mary." And then she did something rather unexpected. She reached into her purse and, from a red wallet, she extracted a five dollar bill and handed it to me. On the reverse side, written in bold black magic marker at the bottom were these words accented by three exclamation points:

"GOD BLESS YOU!!!"

I protested and said: "Please don't give it to me. Please give it to the homeless." And her retort, which still rings in my ears? "No. You are meant to have it."

When I was about to put it into my pocketbook, she said with the deepest heartfelt affection: "I love you!" And, I said the same to her...a total stranger...meeting by chance or by fate?

[<u>Note</u>: I keep the bill in my wallet along with my husband's detective photo.]

Then she gave me a card with her name, (simply "Mary" without a last name showing), and a telephone number printed on it. It quickly joined the five dollar bill to be neatly preserved for a future remembrance.

My newfound friend next began to rise from her seat and she gently grabbed my hands in the process. "I want to pray with you," she said, and then continued. "You work from love. You are bright shining light."

Still holding my hand as we faced eye-to-eye, she comforted my heart with these added words: "Keep doing God's service." And then our hands parted.

No more than a fraction-of-a-fraction-of-a-fraction passed when I twisted my body to retrieve my belongings. Believe me when I tell you that no more than a nanosecond advanced in time...merely a momentary turn of the body before standing upright. And Mary? She was gone! She had seemingly vanished out of thin air!

Remember that I told you that the terminal had clear glass walls everywhere? Well, I could see in all directions measured in merely an instant. And Mary? No where to be seen!

When I was dropped off at the hotel once my ride arrived, I hastily pulled the card out of its hiding place. I needed desperately to try to reconnect to Mary. And when I dialed the number written, a confounding recorded message played: "*This number is not in service.*"

Was Mary connected to the Mary I had prayed to two days before? Was Mary real or imagined? She had to be real because I still have the five dollar bill in my wallet. Was she angelic, a messenger sent by the "Source" to affirm my life's purpose? In my heart-of-hearts, I believe so. Thus, my spiritual healing work continues with a renewed dedication of purpose. And, I gratefully leave you with that parting message.

Epilogue

❦

[**_Postscript:_** After carrying the five dollar bill in my wallet for a lengthy time, I recently was told, by someone who had an inspiring revelation, to look at the serial number written on the currency. Strangely, the thought never occurred to me. And when I looked, I saw the numbers 0281266 grouped together. And the meaning, if any? "028"....my late husband, Dennis, and I were married on the 28th day of August and he was in the 28th Police Precinct. And "1266?" Dennis and I first met in 12 (December) 66 (1966). And after meeting Dennis, I would write on everything, to my mother's expressed annoyance: "Dennis and Lynn...12/1/66...Forever." Did Mary gift the five dollar bill because Dennis needed to reach out to me from **_Beyond the Beyond_**? Is that why I chose to keep it with his detective picture? I'll allow you to supply the answer hoping that you, in the process of wondering, will open your mind and heart to discover the true meaning and purpose of **_YOUR_** life story!]

CPSIA information can be obtained
at www.ICGtesting.com
Printed in the USA
BVHW021522090220
571842BV00022B/1362

9 781977 218476